Putting The Pieces Together

A Practical Guide To Recovery From
Borderline Personality Disorder

Joy A. Jensen

Verona Publishing, Inc.
P.O. Box 24071
Edina, Minnesota 55424

www.veronapublishing.com

2 Putting The Pieces Together

Verona Publishing is pleased to present The Skinny Book, if you are interested in purchasing more copies or if you are interested in books on other topics.

Books can be ordered at www.veronapublishing.com

When ordering in bulk email us the type and number of books required at info@veronapublishing.com

Other books available through Verona Publishing

The Skinny Book, a 6-step methodology for weight management by author, Ayaz Virji, MD.

And in the fiction category a moving story by author Nancy DeRosa, **There's No Place like home**.

Watch for these titles and many more at www.veronapublishing.com or wherever books are sold.

For questions or comments, contact us at info@veronapublishing.com

Cover design by Amanda J. Nichols @ amandanichols.net

Design and layout by Janie Nordberg @ janienordberg@comcast.net

Putting the Pieces Together 2004

Copyright © 2004 by Joy A. Jensen

Published by Verona Publishing, Inc., P.O. Box 24071, Edina, Minnesota 55424

All rights reserved. No part of this book may be reproduced or transmitted in any form or by any means, electronic or mechanical, including but not limited to photocopying, recording or by any information storage and retrieval system, without the prior written permission of the Publisher. Printed in the United States of America.

Library of Congress Cataloging-in-Publication Data:

Library of Congress Control Number: 2004103848

ISBN 0-9667037-6-6

The Wrong Key

She looks at me afraid with pride
Alone in her despair
I gave her all I had inside
She tells me not to care
I am not the chosen one but no one else was there

She turns away my wisdom
She shuts down her mind
Pride must be forsaken
When it makes us blind
A vengeful thought
A word unkind
A broken heart defined
She has got the wisdom
It's all inside her mind

Hating me for giving her
All she ever asked
Baiting me
Attacking me
With words so feebly masked
Experience, for all its worth
Has kept me to my task

Hating me but not forsaking
Again I take the blame
The truth is all she has to see
But still she plays the game
Passion burns inside of me
To her it's all the same

Hating me for knowing
And loving her so well
She'll never forgive me for her private hell
She's afraid to climb back up
Afraid that if she fell
There'd be nothing left inside
There'd be pain until she died
She's got nothing left to hide
It's just all her foolish pride

4 Putting The Pieces Together

Again she looks with pride
Not understanding, fear not withstanding
That life is a choice as is love
Looking for guidance, instead of a high dance
With angels below as above

So I say to her
"Spirit inside you, let living guide you
Please have the strength not to fear
Just look to your spirit
There's no need to fear it
Why wont you please let me near
Surrender your pride to me"

And she says
"I dance alone, I walk the line, sometimes I'm really scared
Superstition, soul division, my vision is impaired
I reach out for your hand and find it is no longer there
I'm the victim of my fate
You're the focus of my hate"

She has the right to happiness
But still she lives in fear
Putting up paper walls
Whenever I get near
She lives inside her house of straw
Disguising all her fear

And I tell myself
"Turn the rage upon her cage
Or let her live in fear
You can win the game you fell into
If you don't interfere
The mask of truth is blinding you to all that you hold dear"

Projecting all her anger
And all her flaws on me
I've not got the patience
It takes to make her see
There's little I can do for her
As long as she hates me

Hoping
Waiting
Wishing her well

Moping
Baiting
"I'll see you in hell!"

I've nothing left to offer
I've nothing left to give
She doesn't want it anyway
I've got a life to live
She owes me no apologies
There's nothing to forgive

If she can shape her dreams
Release her screams, atone
She'll see that we are one
And finally stand alone

And she may never see.

Copyright © 1999-2004 Lukas A. Fragodt. All Rights Reserved.
Unauthorized Duplication Prohibited

Verona Publishing, Inc.
P.O. Box 24071
Edina, Minnesota 55424

www.veronapublishing.com

About the Author

Joy A. Jensen has been an active member of the BPD community since mid-2000. She has been interviewed for an article in JANE magazine, has had poetry published at an online community of artists, Omnigenesis, has contributed to <u>BPDCentral.com</u> for two years, and been associated with <u>BPDResources.com</u>.

A transplant from Grosse Pointe, MI, Joy lives in the foothills of the Rocky Mountains outside of Denver, Colorado with her husband and four dogs.

Ms. Jensen was diagnosed with Borderline Personality Disorder and has fought tirelessly toward recovery.

The ideas and methods expressed in this work represent the opinions of the author only. Before starting any program you should first consult with your doctor. This publication was made to be informative on the topic of Borderline Personality Disorder, but in no way represents a replacement for individualized medical care from your doctor. Neither the publisher nor the author claim any responsibility for liability or harm incurred on the reader secondary to utilization of any of the advice or recommendations of any part of this book.

Certain medical concepts and mechanisms of action of human physiology have been simplified in order to promote understanding for the greatest number of people. By doing this, it is the author's intention not to let medical jargon or complexity interfere with the major points conveyed in this text. It should be understood that the advancement of medical science is based on the development and applications of theoretical principles. These principles are constantly undergoing re-analysis and may change over time as scientific understanding of the particular principle or topic develops and matures.

to

Sharon, for the excellent tools to make this book possible;

to

Al, for the unconditional love with excellent boundaries;

to

Megan, for the terrific, unflappable role model;

to

Lukas, for the primer in living a healthy, happy life;

to

Don, for showing me the essence of acceptance.

8 Putting The Pieces Together

Prologue

Before we get started in this book, I want to take this opportunity to commend you on taking the initiative to work on leading a healthier, happier life. You've taken the first step and you're not alone.

So who am I and what makes me the right person to guide you through some of these processes?

In March, 2000 I sat at my new job, completely paralyzed with fear. I was scared that my life was going to get worse no matter what I did. I was scared of the relationship I had with my boyfriend of almost 6 months. I was scared of love. I was scared of rejection. I was scared of success. I was scared of saying the wrong thing to the wrong person at the wrong time. I was scared of doing the wrong thing at the wrong time with the wrong people. I was petrified of life and of myself, and I felt that I had no one to who I could turn. I felt like whoever I turned to would laugh at me or not understand me at all, and tell me to "pull myself up by my bootstraps." I just knew that if I heard that phrase again, I would become certifiably mad and end up in a straightjacket.

I'd been in and out of therapy since 1982, and it never seemed to "stick." Sure, I'd be temporarily better but then something stressful would happen and I'd slide down to the cellar of depression again. I'd tried medications like Paxil, Xanax and Zoloft for the variations on the seemingly consistent diagnoses of "depression" or "depression with anxiety." Those pills made me feel like a zombie. I had no range of emotion. Life held no particular interest to me and that caused me to swear off medications. After all, no matter what the diagnosis, it was how I was thinking that was causing me to destroy relationships and be suicidal. Mind over matter, right?

The problem wasn't the lack of desire to get "better." The problem was that I didn't know how to get better. One therapist I saw when I was trying to save my marriage pointed out that my husband and

10 Putting The Pieces Together

I were having communication problems. I would scream at him for using paper towels to wipe up a spill rather than using the cheaper paper napkins. I was instructed to use "I" statements and to own my feelings. For example: "I am angry that you're using the 'wrong' paper product."

The use of "I" statements didn't address issues such as my unreasonable expectations, my tendency to flip into unbelievable and scary rages at the drop of a hat, my pervasive feelings of self-worthlessness, or the times I felt extremely disconnected from myself and the world around me. The counselors and therapists I had seen over the years were aware of my feelings and issues because I told them outright at the very beginning of each professional relationship. I was in therapy to get "better," so I saw no point in trying to hide anything from them. My tell-all pattern got to the point where I could meet a new therapist, tell my life story, describe my lifelong trouble areas and still have about twenty minutes left to discuss some of my more immediate concerns.

That day in March, 2000 though, I knew that I needed help and I needed it quickly. I was at a new job and didn't yet have health insurance coverage, but I knew I wouldn't survive another three months with this all-consuming paralytic fear. As fortune would have it, there was a commercial on the radio that day looking for volunteers for a clinical trial for an anti-depressant medication. I called and was accepted into the study within the week. I felt somewhat better at having taken the first step – I had reached out to a professional.

Once in the clinical trial, I took the pills they gave me faithfully and reported to their office every week for a quick evaluation with the nurse administrator, and a not-so-pleasant blood drawing every other week. After nine weeks of the trial and absolutely no changes – good or bad – in my moods, my reactions to stressful situations, my outlook on life, my faith in myself, I found out that I had been on a placebo. The psychiatrist running the clinical trial gave me the actual medication and within three weeks, we determined that the side effects I suffered were outweighing the marginal benefits I was getting. He gave me a physical and an ECT, and then handed me a prescription for Wellbutrin. He told me that this was also marketed as Zyban, the smoking cessation aid. Knowing I was a smoker (at that time, about a pack and a half per day) he told me to take one pill every day for the first week, and cut down on my smoking. Then I was to increase to two pills a day in the second week, and stop smoking entirely by the end of the same week. I laughed.

I've been on Wellbutrin since then with no ill side effects. As a matter of fact, I can barely tell I'm even on a medication. However, those around me can certainly tell if I've skipped a few days of medications, so I would say this is probably the right medication for me. (For the record, some three years later, I'm still a smoker – though I have cut down considerably.)

Although most of my mood swings were under control, I knew that pills alone couldn't "cure" me, and I knew that I should probably check in with a therapist to work on the rest of it. By this time, I had medical coverage through my employer, and I made the requisite calls to the insurance company to track down a therapist. I really didn't care to which school of therapeutic approach they subscribed, what their qualifications were, what gender they were or anything much else about them. I wanted a therapist that was accepting new patients, one that offered a convenient location and who had relatively convenient appointment times open.

I called the first clinic that the Behavior Center at the insurance company offered, and was greeted by an automated directory. I patiently listened to the names and extension numbers and hung up. I called back and listened to the list again and this time jotted down extension numbers of anyone who had a name that sounded "cool" or "intelligent" or basically someone "I could get along with." Then I hung up and called back yet again with my list of extension numbers in-hand. As the automated attendant answered, I punched in the first extension and listened to that therapist's voice mail greeting. I was not impressed, and didn't think I would be able to work with that particular mental health professional. I hung up and called back and dialed in the next extension. I got Sharon's voice mail. I left a message. She called me back the next day and we set an appointment for that Saturday.

My first session with Sharon wasn't much different from my other first sessions with any of the other half-dozen therapists I'd been to. I spilled my life story and glossed over the most urgent topics that I wanted to address. She spent the next twenty minutes asking questions and generally peeking under the surface of what I'd told her. At our next session the following week, toward the end, Sharon looked at me and said, "Well I think I know what the diagnosis is. Would you like to know?" Of course I did! All the other therapists were very cagey about sharing the diagnosis and I'm sure they had what they thought were good reasons. Sharon was able to see right away that I was a woman of action with an inquisitive nature. She told me that I suffered from Borderline Personality Disorder. I sat there somewhat confused. Border-what? What does that mean? What is it?

Rather than trying to explain the disorder to me, she got up and gave me a photocopy of the cover of a book. When I saw the piece of paper, I started to cry. In those six words, I saw my life: "I Hate You, Don't Leave Me"

I went home and ordered the book from Amazon.com, and started scouring the Internet for information on Borderline Personality Disorder (BPD). While my desire for knowledge about my diagnosis was immediate, it was a few months before I took an active role in my own recovery. I needed some time to learn how to recognize BPD in my daily life before I would be able to work on changing those behaviors, let alone deal with the issues causing the behaviors to surface in the first place.

Since my BPD diagnosis just over three years prior to this writing, I have successfully mastered the basic coping techniques that we will discuss within this book and am considered by my therapist, Sharon, and most of the other people I know within the mental health community to be "recovered." In addition to writing this book, I have also created a website devoted to recovering from Borderline Personality Disorder, been very active within the BPD communities on the Internet and have created the most successful BPD recovery discussion board and support community on the Internet. The methods I share in this book are the methods that worked, not only for me, but also for the countless others who have used them to learn how to achieve healthier, happier living.

I wish you much success and happiness in your journey. Please know that you are not alone.

Table of Contents

1 The Optional Chapter 17

2 So You Have BPD 29

3 Is Recovery Possible? 39

4 Do I Need A Therapist? 47

5 Therapeutic Approaches 55

6 Do I Need Medication? 63

7 Mirroring 67

8 The Four Agreements 75

9 Separation of Stuff 81

10 The Five Steps 89

11 Boundaries & Borders 97

12 Letting Go 109

14 Putting The Pieces Together

13 Acceptance 123

14 Self-Talk 131

15 In The Moment 137

16 Self-Harm, Past Trauma, Dissociating & Communication . . .145

17 The Genuine Self 155

18 Goal Setting 161

19 Coping with Crisis Feelings 167

20 Questions & Answers 175

Appendix A – Contracts 197

Appendix B – Support Networks & Resources 215

Appendix C – Acronyms & Definitions 217

Sources 219

16 Putting The Pieces Together

1
The Optional Chapter

When I originally began this book, my primary objective was to provide a set of skills and techniques to help people cope with BPD. Moreover, I wanted to offer a practical guide to recovery from BPD and I was planning to stick entirely to the facts, as I saw them. Over the course of the last eighteen months, mostly during my work on the internet, more and more people have been curious to find out what qualifies me (for lack of a better term) to offer advice on the topic of Borderline Personality Disorder. Because the curiosity level reached a certain point, I thought it might be wise to include a short overview of my life and experiences with BPD and my personal journey to healthy, happy living.

As the main portion of this book was written without this "optional chapter" in existence, it is entirely possible for you, the reader, to skip this chapter in its entirety, if you so choose, without impacting the value of the remaining text. After all, just because I had certain experiences and worked on specific things, those situations may not be relevant to your personal journey in any way. I offer this "optional chapter" for those who'd like to know a little bit more about me and to see that I do, indeed, practice what I 'preach.'

I was born somewhere in Dane County, Wisconsin on November 13, 1971. There are different stories surrounding the first three years of my life. I am adopted, but I was not adopted until just before Christmas in 1974, shortly after my third birthday. My (adoptive) father was and still is a successful florist in Grosse Pointe, Michigan. Around Thanksgiving time, my (foster) grandmother brought me with her to the florist shop to pick up a holiday centerpiece. He was the first person she told that I was available for adoption. I spent that Christmas with my new family.

I remember standing by the fireplace at my great aunt's house, intently focusing on a rather unique ornament. It was ball-shaped, covered in red velvet and had three nooks in which golden cherubs had been placed. From the bottom of the ball was a golden pull which, when pulled, prompted the music to begin and the globe to turn. (Some years later, I ended up with that ornament. It was very special to me because of this first memory.)

I wasn't so much intrigued by the ornament itself as I was trying to figure out my place in this new throng of people who already knew each other. I was the outsider. I didn't belong. I wasn't one of them. I didn't feel comfortable, and I used the ornament as a distraction, trying to "play it off" and pretend that I wasn't uncomfortable and insecure. My Borderline probably started that very day, December 24th, 1974.

My (adoptive) mother told me some twenty years later that following the adoption, my parents wanted to take me back to my foster grandparents' home for a visit and dinner. Apparently, I threw quite the temper tantrum and had to be soundly spanked and disciplined before I pulled together and acted like a big girl. Looking back, it's obvious to me that I was petrified that I had done something horrible, that I wasn't good enough, that I needed to be returned. Rather than acknowledging these childish but still realistic fears, my new family punished me. After all, a spanking means punishment – at least to a three year old.

I'm sure quite a few of us heard some of these phrases while growing up:

- If you don't stop crying, I'll give you something to cry about.
- Children should be seen and not heard.
- Quit your crocodile tears.
- If you know what's good for you, you'll keep your mouth closed.
- Do as I say, not as I do.
- Do not speak unless spoken to.

Or perhaps these were things that were inherent only to my own childhood. Over the years, I learned that to be good, I needed to be quiet, respectful and obedient. In my pre-teen years, as my parents were going through their divorce, I was sent to a very nice, caring family therapist to make sure that I wasn't being adversely affected by the somewhat hostile proceedings. I distinctly recall mentioning that I could usually predict my mother's mood based on her hair style for the day. When it was down, she would be nice, affectionate and caring. When it was up or pulled back, look out! Those were the days she usually had a headache, and it seemed nothing I could do would ever be good enough.

Growing up, I felt like I was continuously walking on eggshells. One slip of the tongue, one perceived disrespectful look, or not moving quickly enough were all causes for punishment. The rules I was expected to play by were never consistent. I knew that I was not to speak unless spoken to, that I should always say please and thank you, that I should never say "What?" in response to someone's question if I hadn't heard them clearly, and that I should never ask for anything but instead wait for it to be offered to me. Looking back, I realize I was constantly trying to predict what was expected of me: whether I was allowed to speak, whether I should be honest in terms of really saying what I felt or thought, or risk the wrath of being called a liar. I was always seeking the path of least resistance and attempting to keep from rocking the boat. My life was all about keeping a low profile and as such, I didn't really have, or allow myself the opportunity to feel the way toward my genuine self.

I lived in a lot of different homes as a child. By the time I left for college at the age of sixteen, I had lived in eleven homes. We moved with great regularity, and I never really minded because each move meant I got a whole new room. Not just a new floor plan but a whole new design scheme. One room was cornflower blue and white, and another was lavender irises with rose colored carpet. My father had an eye for fixer-uppers, and he could usually make a tidy profit with each fix-and-flip. The only down side to the regular moves was that the homes were rarely in a neighborhood with children my age. I didn't have any friends to speak of until my second year of high school. I didn't have friends to talk with on the phone, compare gossip with, or do homework with. I never went bike riding or swimming at the local park with friends. I usually stayed at home, alone, with my books and assorted other things to keep me occupied.

Once, we moved next door to a house filled with kids. The Koch children were my idea of perfect at that time. They were all tan, athletic, boisterous and light-hearted. I think my mother saw them differently: low-class, dirty, obnoxious, and crude. I don't think any of the four children ever set foot inside our house; not once in the three years we lived next door to them. I did have fun when I was hanging out with Joey, Amy, Molly and Ben. It was neat to see what a real girl's bedroom looked like – with toys, dolls, contemporary things on the walls like the Karen Carpenter poster – rather than what I'd grown up with, as if I lived in an Architectural Digest child's room. Nothing personal was ever present, as I recall. Sure, I had toys like Lego blocks and games like Merlin and Simon and Scrabble but no Barbie dolls. My room at the house next to the Koch's was done in yellows and whites. I had some antique furniture in there which always made me nervous. I had to be especially careful around them because they were precious pieces of furniture. Any decorations on the walls were tastefully chosen artistic pieces that matched the décor rather than anything that one might consider suitable for a ten year old little girl.

Life was extremely regimented when I was growing up. Rise and shine, followed by the morning bathroom rituals, getting dressed for school (a private Catholic institution requiring a uniform, leaving no room for personal choice or individual freedom) followed by making the bed complete with hospital corners. Breakfast was served at the table, not the breakfast bar, and every last bite had to be consumed. I was raised on 2% milk and one day my mother ran out of it. I sat down for cereal and was surprised by the half-and-half that covered my Corn Flakes. I was unaccustomed to the taste and didn't care for it. I ate very slowly, and this was a cause for concern for my mother who then told me when to take each bite until the entire bowl was empty.

I'm sure that by this point, my childhood seems very bleak. That's not entirely true, and I don't paint this picture to gain sympathy. I illustrate these points to set the stage for the Borderline issues with which I'd have to contend later in life.

I got the best of both worlds from my parents. My father was a free spirit, generous and very supportive but not very disciplined, especially when it came to finances. My mother was quite the opposite, and it was fitting that she became a teacher with her fondness for discipline, structure and focus. I learned to take the best of both of them and make those traits my own. I'm sure, though, that most of my Obsessive Compulsive tendencies come from my mother's love for complete order and organization.

As I got into high school, following my parents divorce, I was still trying to figure out who I was. I had no friends as I was growing up, and since I went to private Catholic schools until college, anyone I might have been friends with didn't live nearby. I grew up as an only child, the youngest of all cousins, painfully shy and still waiting for others to speak to me so that I could be allowed to speak to them. I didn't know the first thing about how to behave outside of adults. In the presence of my parents' friends, I was the precious, darling, adorable little angel. I was called precocious and complimented on my looks and intelligence. I skipped second grade, so I was also the oddity among my classmates for a very long time because they assumed I was super smart. I found out later that I had been double-promoted at my mother's insistence since she herself had been double-promoted as a young girl.

At one point, I prided myself on being able to be friendly with just about anyone in my high school. I could pass time with the girls who were laughed about because their family shopped at discount stores. I could joke around and laugh with the popular, pretty, athletic girls. I couldn't play sports with them or date like them, but they never turned their backs to me if I showed up. I could also meld with the "stoners" even though I'd never touched or even seen a drug in my life. I was the consummate chameleon. And I was proud of it. I thought that it made me special and talented that I could shift who I was at any given time, and I thought it made me cooler, more popular, more liked by a greater number of people. I didn't realize that my transience was a reflection of my own unstable sense of self.

I actually had a cycle of mini-self-destructions beginning in third grade. Apparently I didn't feel challenged by the work that we were required to do each day in our workbooks, so instead of just doing the work, I would scribble and doodle. At year's end, I spent the summer erasing all of that and completing the work as had been previously assigned. I straightened up and flew right for fourth grade, but by fifth grade, I was up to my old tricks. This time I just wouldn't do the homework. It got to the point that I had thirty-eight missing homework assignments. When my mother found out, I was spanked thirty-eight times on each buttock with a wooden meat tenderizer. And then I was given an assignment book – a day planner – in which I was required to make note of all my homework requirements and then obtain each teacher's signature or initials. Sixth grade was a breeze and I must have done well in seventh and eighth grades too because the next mini-meltdown wasn't until freshman year of high school. I wasn't entirely sure of how I was doing academically, and my dad was headed off to Parent-Teacher conferences. He asked me how I was doing and I didn't want to say "A's and B's" just in case I wasn't doing that well so I underestimated my scores to "low B's, mostly C's and probably a D." My dad hit the roof because he'd trusted me to do well on my own, unsupervised. I was so distraught that I went upstairs and swallowed as many aspirin as I could find in a ludicrous attempt to kill myself. All my life I'd been taught (through words and actions) that I was smart. I certainly wasn't personable since I didn't have any friends, so if smart was all I had and now I wasn't smart enough to be loved and accepted, then there really wasn't any point to living.

I was very black-and-white that evening. As I sat on the floor of the darkened hallway, crying into my dog Sandy's fur, the pendulum began to swing back the other way. I didn't want to die. I really didn't. I picked up the phone and called one of the girls I knew at school and asked if her mother could take me to the hospital. I hated life but I didn't want to leave it. I just wanted the pain stop and I didn't know how to make that happen.

I mentioned previously that I started college when I was sixteen years old. I was so anxious to get away and spread my wings. I was eager to discover who I could really become. I wanted to get as far away as I possibly could. I chose to go to Western Michigan University, about one hundred and fifty miles from home, even though my father really wanted me to attend Nazareth College, also the same distance from home but much smaller. WMU had a student population of about 10,000 at that time, whereas Nazareth College had an average class size of about 750 students and it was, of course, a Catholic college with a very protected environment. I believed I mentioned that my father was supportive and he truly was, and still is. He was willing to let me learn my own lessons, through my own mistakes, regardless of how messy I could make things.

About two months into my first semester at WMU, I came home for a long-weekend. A former high school classmate was attending Ohio State University. They had Columbus Day as a holiday, so I figured I'd go home and have some fun while she was in town. On my way back to WMU, I ended up meeting a guy. Or, to be more precise: a man. I was still sixteen and this man was twenty seven. We dated for quite some time, and I ended up moving in with him, in Chicago, after I dropped out of school.

He wasn't the cause of my slipping grades at school. In fact, we only saw each other about twice a month. The simple fact of the matter was that I was too young to be out on my own. I didn't have the desire to self-discipline any longer. I was spreading my wings and free-falling to dangerous lows. I even ended up in the hospital one night as a result of having too much to drink. It wasn't so much the alcohol that landed me in the emergency room as it was the fall I took, the cut I sustained and the blood I was leaking all over my dorm room. Apparently I was a belligerent drunk and took a couple of swings at the cops and paramedics trying to get me onto the gurney. When I returned to conscious awareness of my surroundings, I immediately became devious and plotted escape twice. I even managed to get myself back to the campus after the second, and successful, attempt where, after a hot shower, I was escorted back to the police station to wait to be released into my father's custody.

About seven years later, I was in a very similar situation but I was mature enough by that time to keep it from escalating to the point of medical intervention. I was in an abusive relationship with a man over ten years my senior. We had just broken up – due, in large part, to my "craziness" – and had begun seeing another woman. This woman was very similar to me. We were about the same height, weight and build with the same hair and eye color. The main difference was that she was closer to his age and already had a daughter. I found out during the course of our rocky break-up that she was a drug user.

My intense anger at that time was because one part of me saw the physical similarities between her and me. The thought occurred to me that he was looking for a "replacement me." But then her lifestyle choices and ordinary conduct were the polar opposite of what I identified to be my own choices and conduct. In retrospect, it would seem that my anger was multi-pronged:

He was rejecting me as a person, life partner choice and as a woman.

He was choosing someone completely different from me without affording me the opportunity to change myself to become what it seemed he wanted.

I had no further control over the fate of the relationship.

I had run out of chances to maintain a relationship with him and that was inconsistent with our history of "push-and-pull."

One day, she came over to our apartment to go out with my ex-boyfriend and I stayed in my room because I didn't want to see her. Sure enough, I had to look out the window to watch them walking toward his car, hand-in-hand. I lost it. I flew into an absolute fit of Borderline rage. I was screaming out the window at them and whoever happened to be home in the nearly-one hundred other apartments in the area surely heard me. I wasn't satisfied with my screaming because neither one of them would look back at me, let alone engage in a screaming match, which was my goal.

24   Putting The Pieces Together

Once they were off the premises, I felt an overwhelming need to make him really suffer. I knew that he liked his bedroom to be very dark during the day so that he could take a nap when he got home from his job. I had selected, bought and installed the room-darkening navy drapes on his bedroom windows. I went to the kitchen, got a butcher knife and proceeded to slash his drapes to shreds.

In my mind, at the time, my actions were perfectly reasonable. My goal was to get him to see that I was better than this new woman, that he should dump her and come back to me. If I couldn't get him to do that, I wanted him to acknowledge my pain and absolute heartache for his cavalier attitude toward replacing me so quickly. I wanted him to shout and yell and be violent right back because it would show me that he still had some compassion toward me. He was hurting me. He was replacing me. He was leaving me.

The catch to this whole thing was that I was the one who broke up with him in the first place. I had become disillusioned by his failure to live up to my expectations of perfection. He had fallen from the pedestal on which I placed him very early on in our long-distance relationship. Once I moved in with him – I was 19, he was 28 – I began to see the real man. There wasn't necessarily anything terribly bad about who he was, but he wasn't the guy I'd built up in my mind with smoke and mirrors. I resented him a great deal for not being my idea of perfection and felt betrayed, as though I'd been lied to. The truth is that I had been deceived; by myself rather than by him. I was too wrapped up in my Borderline twisted thinking to realize that I was the one leading the tango. It was much easier to pin the blame on him rather than accept the responsibility for my own warped initial view of him. Once I finished playing The Blame Game and came out the winner, no blame to be found on my side, it was time to retaliate for the hurt he inflicted.

To the two of them, I surely must have looked like a raving lunatic. Here's a woman who breaks up with her boyfriend because he never managed to live up to these wild ideas of the "perfect boyfriend," and now she's screaming out the window at the top of her lungs and shredding drapes with a butcher knife. I think we can all agree that these are not the acts of a rational person.

Because of the nearly complete emotional breakdown as the result of the break-up with this man, I was despondent and felt that I had nothing left worth living for. I had no pets to care for, no man who cared for me, family that I'd left behind in another state and a peon job that didn't amount to much at all in terms of prestige or pay. I felt hopeless and helpless and didn't initially see any way around or out of that stage.

I sat alongside the bathtub (because I didn't want to be found naked), on a large plastic bag (to make clean-up easier once I was complete), had the warm water running (to ease the pain of cutting) and a large kitchen knife in-hand. I was sobbing like a fiend and angry at the same time. I, once again, didn't want to die but I also didn't want the pain to continue. I focused on the guy rather than on my own thoughts and issues. With intense concentration and the center of my attention on this guy – who was verbally and physically abusive – I suddenly came to the realization that he was scum. Maybe that's too strong a word to use to describe someone and perhaps I should also apologize for the many years I nicknamed him "Asshole" but it was a coping mechanism that I glommed onto and it buoyed me for quite some time. By labeling him the bad guy and viewing him as a lesser form of life, I could justify to myself that my life was worth more than his and, as such, I would be letting him "win" if I followed through on my suicide plan.

Once I resolved to keep living and regain "the upper hand" in the twisted relationship, I turned off the water, stopped crying, put the knife back in the kitchen and threw away the plastic bag. My hurt, sadness and pain had turned to anger which fueled my desire and ability to see my way through the pain and back into happy (if not healthy) living.

A short time after that evening, I went to the company Christmas party – stag. I was very much "anti-male" at that point in my life. Rather than being able to acknowledge my own issues or even look within for any meaningful answers, I pointed the finger toward an entire gender and carried that Montana-sized chip on my shoulder with (misplaced) pride. At that party, though, I danced with a guy. Compared to the former boyfriend who was overweight and preferred to spend hours at a stretch at the local dive-of-a-bar, this was something very different for me.

As I got to know this man over the next couple of months, I realized he was the polar opposite of the abusive one. He was meek, mild-mannered and considerate. I figured that if I was miserable with the overbearing, domineering and powerful force-of-personality, it stood to reason that I would be tickled pink to be with someone the exact opposite. We were married nine months after we first started dating.

26   Putting The Pieces Together

Through both of these relationships, I never once addressed the inner issues. I was still looking for external validation. I was still looking for love from another person without yet being able to love myself. While it would be easy to point the finger and blame the handful of therapists for not forcing me to do so, the responsibility ultimately rested with me. I continually gave up on therapy. I never requested alternate approaches.

Almost four years into my marriage, we both realized that we were having some serious problems. We went to marriage counseling with the same therapist I'd had when my own parents divorced. Perhaps that was a mistake because of the prior relationship. Perhaps it was my way to control the situation by having that added edge of prior experience with her. At the time, I chalked it up to not knowing any other therapists in the area that dealt with these sorts of issues – which was, in part, true.

About two months – or four sessions – into our marriage counseling, we stopped going due to financial considerations. About two months after that, I made a solo appointment with the therapist. I was in tears for the whole session as I told her how I felt horrible that I was starting to think my marriage was unsalvageable. Not for lack of trying, mind you, but because we were inherently different people and totally unsuited for each other. "He was a dreamer; I was a doer." As a person of action, I was constantly aggravated by someone who would sit back and wistfully opine about what could be rather than actually doing anything to make those dreams come true. There was no reason to think that either of us could change who we were, and that made me miserable because I was terribly afraid to be seen as a failure, through my divorce. Plus, he and I had sworn to each other in many conversations that we would not get divorced, that we would do whatever it took to stay together. It felt like double-failure.

Lo and behold, it seemed that my husband didn't hold as tightly to those vows as I had. I may, of course, be mistaken and it could just be that he handled the situation better than I did. My solitary appointment with the counselor was on a Saturday morning while he was at work. He got home at 1pm and I initiated the discussion about divorce and mediation. He told me that mediation wasn't needed, that all he wanted was his clothes, his clubs, his cards and his car. By 8am that Monday morning, his car was packed up and he was on his way back to his dad's house, three hundred miles away.

The Optional Chapter   27

I still joke that it took me nine months and $45,000 to get married, but only thirty days and $600 to get divorced. Our divorce was possibly the most amicable one on record, especially taking into consideration the ups-and-downs we had during the course of the four year marriage.

Once he moved out of the house, I started getting online and into chat rooms. I stumbled into a metaphysical chat room and was amazed. I felt alive for the first time in a very long while. There were challenging questions, existential and philosophical discussions and topics in general that really made me think and exercise my brain. It felt wonderful. As part of that newly found euphoria, I also managed to begin flexing my femaleness in terms of sexuality. I never spoke to any of the women in the chat community and was a consummate flirt or tease to virtually every man I encountered.

Turning a long story into a shorter one, I ended up chatting with a guy who lived in the same state as my cousin - Colorado. I was planning a trip out there for my birthday and he offered to let me sit in on his tae kwon do classes. I accepted the offer and thought very little about it, as my attention was still on some other guy that I would be visiting with during my trip. As time passed and my trip grew closer, my communication with the original guy tapered off while my conversations with the martial arts instructor increased, eventually progressing to telephone conversations.

During the entire development of our relationship, from Day One, I knew he was married. At the beginning, I jokingly asked if his wife would mind my sitting in on his tae kwon do classes. As we progressed into more intimate telephone conversations, I recall telling him – as he expressed doubts and hesitation about the sanity of the two of us getting involved – that, "before this is over, there will be a lot of tears and heartache but this is something that I'm willing to go ahead with because I feel like I need to." I had a semi-subconscious belief that I needed to suffer in order to fully and truly learn.

While this relationship was developing deeper and getting more entangled in my heart and psyche, I became attracted to another man. Initially, my goal was merely competitive because whenever he showed up in the chat room, all the women fawned all over him. Recognition from him was a treat. At least, that's how it seemed to me. I was bound and determined to get in on that. Once I managed to gain a glimmer of recognition, we started talking on a deeper level and my fascination with him grew.

Both men were aware of my interest in the other and, naturally, both were telling me to dump the other one. No matter what the second guy said to me – how I was cheating myself out of a real, genuine, loving relationship with the married guy – I was unwilling to let go of that triangle, still insistent that I was required to see it through to the end so that I could fully absorb the lessons intended for me.

Again, in the interest of making this story easier to digest, I'll cut to the chase. I ended up dumping the truly caring guy, and saw it out to the bitter end with the married guy. About a year after I had last spoken to the compassionate guy, we "spoke" again online. It was shortly after I had received the diagnosis of Borderline and I was just getting started in my journey of recovery. That was three years ago. We are now friends, and he has started a family with another friend of mine.

A great many of the things he tried to get me to understand very early on in our association, I simply wasn't ready to hear, absorb, understand or accept. Now, though, some of those very same edicts have become the backbone of my genuine self and daily life. As I took more and more steps toward my future – healthy, happy living – each new thing I learned related in some way back to the wisdom he had previously tried to impart to me. I was too stubborn, pig-headed and immature at the time to recognize the tremendous value in his words. They were more than mere words; they were a prescription for living. Instead of taking that prescription to a pharmacist so I could get it filled, I threw it away for a year. It wasn't until I had a starting point – a diagnosis that made sense – that I was able to see the value in that prescription.

So what sorts of things did he share with me? Well, they're covered in this book, for the most part. They're not outlined or highlighted with bullet points; they're more subtle than that. They are overall theories and applications of how to effectively live with boundaries or borders to achieve that healthy, happy living that we all crave – and have the potential to achieve.

So You Have BPD

Whether you've been formally diagnosed, or you ran across something on the internet, in a newspaper or magazine article, or saw it portrayed in a movie and recognized yourself, you need to know that BPD is a real disorder and it is possible to recover from it and learn to function in a healthy way.

"How do others see me?" There are plenty of books and websites chock-full of horror stories. Even some movies portray some pretty wild characterizations of Borderline. One of the most common reactions I've seen in my years of experience with Borderlines working toward recovery is a state of shock at how the outside world perceives a Borderline's actions. What we might inherently know or recognize to be "I'm just hurting so much on the inside that I have to make you feel it too so you'll understand," the person on the outside of the disorder may have come to the conclusion that such actions are irrational and socially unacceptable.

So what can be done? Should we focus our energies on trying to make 'the outside world' understand what it's like to live with a Borderline mind? Most certainly NOT! Our energies should be focused on regaining control over our actions, retraining our thought processes and getting ourselves to the state of healthy, happy living.

I do think, however, that it is beneficial to take some time to examine how others may have perceived us, so that we may add to our library of acceptable and unacceptable social behaviors. Only by being cognizant of what has and has not worked in the past are we prepared to face the challenge of leading a Borderline-free life.

The DSM-IV Diagnostic Criteria for Borderline Personality Disorder

If you haven't already perused the DSM-IV Diagnostic Criteria for BPD, you will find it excerpted in here for quick review.

DMS-IV Diagnostic Criteria

A person who suffers from this disorder has labile interpersonal relationships characterized by instability. This pattern of interacting with others has persisted for years and is usually closely related to the person's self-image and early social interactions. The pattern is present in a variety of settings (e.g., not just at work or home) and often is accompanied by a similar liability (fluctuating back and forth, sometimes in a quick manner) in a person's affect, or feelings. Relationships and the person's affect may often be characterized as being shallow. A person with this disorder may also exhibit impulsive behaviors and exhibit a majority of the following symptoms:

- frantic efforts to avoid real or imagined abandonment.
- a pattern of unstable and intense interpersonal relationships characterized by alternating between extremes of idealization and devaluation
- identity disturbance: markedly and persistently unstable self-image or sense of self
- impulsivity in at least two areas that are potentially self-damaging (e.g., spending, sex, substance abuse, reckless driving, binge eating)
- recurrent suicidal behavior, gestures, or threats, or self-mutilating behavior
- affective instability due to a marked reactivity of mood (e.g., intense episodic dysphoria, irritability, or anxiety usually lasting a few hours and only rarely more than a few days)
- chronic feelings of emptiness
- inappropriate, intense anger or difficulty controlling anger (e.g., frequent displays of temper, constant anger, recurrent physical fights)
- transient, stress-related paranoid ideation or severe dissociative symptoms

Criteria summarized from: American Psychiatric Association. (1994). *Diagnostic and statistical manual of mental disorders, fourth edition.* Washington, DC: American Psychiatric Association.

Many of us recognize our behavior within the diagnostic criteria. Some of us will resonate with five of the criteria; others will strike a chord with all nine to varying degrees of severity. To our knowledge, no relationship between the number of diagnostic criteria attributed to the person with BPD, and their prospects for recovery has been established. This means that recovery isn't dependent upon, nor is it subject to, a specific level of disorder in ones life.

How do you recognize BPD in your daily life?

There are many terms that will be discussed within this guide that may sound like pop-psychology but are quite useful when discussing the ways in which BPD rears its ugly head.

Fear of Abandonment

Fear of abandonment seems to be the most prevalent of the BPD traits, and often crops up in the most unexpected places. Intimate relationships are traditionally expected to have some element of fear of abandonment within them. In today's society of skyrocketing divorce rates, it has been ingrained into our heads that relationships don't last. Perhaps we might feel justified knowing that we have a history of tumultuous relationships that didn't last beyond a certain threshold. Some folks claim that ten years is their benchmark, others say four; and still others have yet to make it to the one-year mark in any given relationship.

Fear of abandonment shows itself in more than romantic relationships though. We see it in friendships – both real life and internet based. We see it in familial and sibling relationships. We see it in professional relationships. About the only place we don't see it is in relationships with pets. In just about any human-to-human relationship, however, we fear that at some point we won't be good enough to keep this other person in our lives.

Sadly, more often than not, we are caught in a vicious cycle of self-fulfilling prophecy. Only through recovery are we able to break out of that cycle and begin to have healthy relationships and interactions.

Triggers

Scattered throughout the ever-growing amount of literature on the subject of BPD is the term "triggers," meaning those things that set us off, or trigger our erratic behaviors. Just about anything under the sun can be a trigger. Triggers are completely dependent upon the person perceiving them. Experiences are filtered, at all times, through our individual perceptions, and usually run through our experiences to determine several things such as: relevancy, urgency, threat and traditional response.

A disordered childhood or traumatic experience in our lives can seriously skew the way in which we filter experiences and apply meaning to them. Recovery is about learning to adjust and fine-tune our filtering mechanisms and respond to situations that may have once triggered us into a full-blown rage, or sent us spiraling into the abysmal depths of depression in a healthier way.

Red-Lining

If you've ever watched the needle on a speedometer in a vehicle rise and fall as a result of the pressure the driver applies to either the gas or brake pedals, you have the basic understanding of the term "red-lining." More often than not, a speedometer has a black background with white numbers and hash marks. Toward the higher end of the speedometer, the numbers and hash marks may be red to indicate that you might be operating the vehicle at an unsafe speed. The red lines are there to warn of danger.

We've all seen movies of drag racing and probably even witnessed (if not engaged in it ourselves) trying to "beat someone off the line" as a red light turns green. These drivers take their foot off the brake pedal and "floor it" to go as fast as they can, as quickly as they can. Given the right vehicle the driver can red-line in a matter of seconds.

This is the same principle in many cases of BPD. The Borderline often sees a situation (or a trigger) and responds to it like a drag racer responds to a green light: they floor it and are red-lining in no time.

Black-and-White

With very few (if any) exceptions, most of us have learned to think in black-and-white. There is no grey in the our world. There is good or evil. There is euphoria or depression. There is love or hate. There is right or wrong.

Because the black-and-white thinking is so pervasive, it is one of the hardest obstacles to overcome. We become so accustomed to things being a certain way, to viewing the world through black-and-white glasses that we have a difficult time letting go of the old ways of thinking and viewing the world around us. One of the primary goals of recovery is to introduce grey into the black-and-white world and make the concept comfortable to us.

Pedestals

Along with black-and-white thinking, we often have put people in our lives on pedestals. Soon these people tumble down, and we hate them for not living up to certain standards. Pedestals are primary culprits in the unstable relationships we often encounter.

Take a look at the series of illustrations in the Appendix which have been excerpted from "Different Dances" by Shel Silverstein for a representation of placing individuals on pedestals.

Splitting

Splitting is a term that is used to describe how we generally view loved ones in our lives. Oftentimes, when we meet a new person, we place that person on a pedestal and idolize them. That person is wonderful, the epitome of perfection, they can do no wrong. This perception of perfection is the "white" of black-and-white thinking. The pedestal is actually comprised of all the ideals that the we wish that person would bring into our lives, and not the real virtues the person does or does not bring to the relationship.

Because the black-and-white thinking is so ingrained and pervasive in our world, it becomes nearly impossible for us to understand how someone who was once so perfect could suddenly be so tainted, flawed, imperfect. There can be no co-existence of black-and-white, good-and-bad, perfect-and-flawed in the world of Borderline. The idealized person can no longer be one complete, whole, human being capable of grey; they must (by black-and-white definition) be two separate entities.

The good person, we love and adore and cherish. The bad person, we hate, despise and revile. If we see one tiny hint of imperfection (as defined by the standards of perfection of that person's BPD-made pedestal), then they can no longer be ALL GOOD so therefore they must be ALL BAD, and we hate them immensely for many reasons – betrayal, fraud, abandonment, rejection, etc.

However, as is often the case, after red-lining and going off in a full-blown rage at the split person, two possibilities exist: 1.) we feel stupid for not seeing the person's treachery in the first place, and we write the person out of our lives; or 2.) we soften and the person's good actions come back to our memory, and they become good again.

So now what do you think?

Having read the DSM-IV Diagnostic Criteria and read a little bit about some of the terms that will be used in this guide, what do you think about your chances for recovery? Are you feeling hopeful and energized? Or are you feeling that there is an insurmountable mountain before you?

Human beings are amazing and resilient creatures. The capacity for learning, growing and healing is remarkable. Please don't give up hope.

You're not alone and you can do this!

Where does it come from?

Nature versus nurture is a long-standing debate in almost all behavioral aspects of the human being and it won't be answered in this guide but it is beneficial to have the discussion as a starting point to understanding the origin of BPD.

There are those that firmly believe that BPD is genetic simply because the characteristics are so universal that it would be statistically impossible to have people from differing socio-economic and family situations develop the exact same traits. In other words, it would be impossible for me to teach someone how to be Borderline.

The proponents of the nature theory are correct in assuming that an inner city, poor child would have any similarities to an upper-middle class child. Without having similar family structure and daily interactions and activities, it's almost impossible to say that it is a child's environment that causes them to develop BPD.

Yet, most of the material related to BPD centers around the behavioral aspects of the patient, the Borderline. The texts address the Borderline's ability to think, be cognitively aware, understand and appreciate the passage of time, to identify with core aspects of themselves. Because of the effectiveness of behavior modification programs, those in the nurture camp believe that BPD is something that's learned over time since it can be unlearned through certain therapeutic approaches.

That the child who develops Borderline is genetically predisposed to certain mood disorders is more likely since BPD is most often co-morbid—rarely seen as a stand-alone disorder—and that in certain cases, the nurturance provided within the young child's life can teach the child how to effectively cope.

While many, if not most, Borderlines are able to point to their parents, or even more specifically their mothers, as some root causes to their inability to effectively deal with their feelings, parenting abilities may not be the sole culprit. There is a non-zero portion of the Borderline population that believes their childhood within the family unit was healthy but that their trauma came from peers. Merciless teasing at school, being picked on, getting called names can all serve to undermine a child's sense of self during the vulnerable period when they begin to try to fit in and be accepted.

Am I a freak?

Many times people who have been recently diagnosed with BPD believe themselves to be freakish because of the diagnosis. They read the DSM-IV Diagnostic Criteria and are appalled that they're so abnormal that there's an entire disorder about them. Yet, for other people, receiving the diagnosis is a saving grace. It's usually a godsend for those individuals who've spent years in and out of therapy, trying different medications, grasping at straws, berating themselves for not being able to pull themselves up by their own bootstraps because there is finally "a reason to be." Finally they have an explanation for the craziness; a definable disorder, and for a lot of individuals knowing the origin of the issues is the first step in changing the patterns.

No, in short, having BPD does not make a person a sideshow freak worthy of a tent at the circus. However, as with just about any mental illness, there is invariably some hesitation on the part of the general population when hearing that someone they know has a mental disorder. Later in this guide, we'll discuss who to tell, and when and how to tell them, but for now, let's examine this:

> *"Whether you believe that you are a freak or whether you believe that you are not a freak, you are correct."*

The above phrase has been adapted for the purposes of this discussion to emphasize the power of belief. Our thoughts have enormous power and potential in our lives. It is our thoughts that define who we are, what we believe and the actions we take.

Many times, we do something klutzy or air-headed. But a single event or occurrence over the course of a lifetime doesn't define us as a klutz or an airhead. Similarly, maybe reading the DSM-IV Diagnostic Criteria made some folks feel uncomfortable or freakish, but that is just a temporary feeling and does not define the entire person.

The positive side of BPD

There are many who view having a diagnosis of a mental illness as a death knell, that nothing good will ever happen for them, that the world will always treat them like a doddering fool. Again, the power of thought is an amazing thing and this guide would be incomplete if the positive aspects of the disorder weren't discussed.

> *"The unexamined life is not worth living."*
> *~ Aristotle*

One of the biggest and most rewarding benefits of Borderline is the work it takes to look within and get to know yourself. Okay, so maybe that doesn't sound like a benefit so much as it sounds like an awful lot of hard work. It's both. The hard work is required to overcome the Borderline, however, the payoff is astronomical insofar as it provides the one who comes out the other end of the BPD tunnel with insight and awareness that most ordinary "healthy" people don't achieve.

Think about it. Pick fifteen people you know and if you were to ask them to define themselves, do you think they would be able to do it? If you were to ask them to pick three personality traits and discuss how those things came to be a part of who they are today, and what the benefits of those traits are, do you think they'd be able to hold an intelligent discussion?

The truth is that the process of overcoming BPD is one of the most personally enriching things you'll ever do. Most children simply grow up and don't think twice about it. Those of us with Borderline age but don't grow up until we hit the recovery phase of our lives – and hopefully we get to that point before we die. It is during our growing up phase as adults that we are better able to understand the world around us, to really get to know who we are, what we respect and admire, how we can become the people we've always wanted to be. Children who go through this process at the age of three or six or ten or fifteen simply don't have the cognitive awareness to examine their lives and take an active stance in determining who they will become.

The layout of this guide

We're not even out of the first chapter of recovery-oriented material yet and you're already aware that recovery is hard work. A book is not a magic wand, and merely reading this text or any handful of other books won't make the Borderline simply vanish. It will take hard work and effort on your part. You have years of learned behavior to unlearn and new techniques to learn in place of the unhealthy ones, and you'll need to practice them until they become second-nature to you.

At the end of each chapter, there will be homework. You won't be sending in the homework. You won't be getting graded on the homework. There won't be anyone standing over you to make sure you do the homework. The homework is optional. However, if you skip over the exercises, you're only cheating yourself.

You bought this book because you wanted to make a difference in your life. You bought this book because you wanted to learn more about yourself and your disorder. You bought this book because you want things to change in your life.

There is a cause-and-effect relationship in recovery. You need to take action in order to see results. The homework won't always be easy and you may not want to pick up this guide for a couple of days while you work through some of the feelings that come up when you do an exercise. That's okay. Just remember that your recovery is in your own hands, that you have enormous power to effect change over your life and who you are. This is your golden opportunity to become who you've always wanted to be.

38 Putting The Pieces Together

Throughout this guide, there will also be some inserts from other Borderlines, including me. You are not alone, nor are you the only one who's experienced these things. However, since every person's situation is unique; the main focus is and will remain your own journey to recovery.

Homework

These exercises are very limited in scope for this chapter. You will be drawing more upon them further into the guide. For now, you are asked to simply identify the behaviors.

- List three times you acted upon black-and-white thinking. How did that work out for you? What do you think you could have done to handle the situation differently? To achieve a more successful outcome?

- Write about someone you placed on a pedestal. What sort of things did you tend to ignore when you elevated them in your mind? What happened when you realized that they were not that idealized person? How did you feel? Do you notice any trends – the basic relationship in which you generally put people on a pedestal, the types of things you initially overlook, etc.?

- List three things that scare you in a relationship. Do you have any idea how to overcome those fears? (It's okay if you don't just yet. That will come as you make progress in your journey.)

- Write about someone you split. How were you feeling at the time? How did you feel later, after the heat of the moment subsided?

Is Recovery Possible?

First of all, yes, recovery is indeed possible. Most of us have a basic concept of recovery from BPD as living like a "normal" person, not blowing up all the time, not living on a roller coaster, having stable relationships, not being self-destructive or many other things that are the opposite of our current lives.

Is there such a thing as "true recovery"?

There are many arguments of semantics floating around about recovery. Some camps say that the basic thought processes are still present in people who have learned to lead healthier lives, and therefore recovery hasn't happened – that the Borderline has simply learned to work around the problem which still exists.

Others argue that by disassembling the old coping strategies and erasing the old negative self-talk tapes, replacing the strategies with healthier ones and rerecording the tapes with positive and healthy statements and beliefs, the Borderline itself will be excised and replaced – much like a home renovation.

Another group argues, logically, that recovery implies a return to a particular state, condition or level of functionality. Yet, in the case of Borderline, we never had that level of functionality in the first place. Granted, it is possible to do the work to achieve a healthy, happy life but we do not return to a level of health like a former cancer patient might. We simply continue to grow and learn and improve ourselves to a point we had not previously achieved.

We won't get into nitty-gritty debates over the usage of words or their literal meanings. This guide is about getting off the roller coaster, retraining the brain into accepting the grey of the world, ascertaining your genuine self, putting the shattered pieces back together and living a healthier, happier life.

Regardless of which theory you may subscribe to, you still have the capacity to learn new things and become a healthier person. Labels are rampant in this world, and many times people get caught up in their labels. Rather than focusing on the ultimate goal – healthy, happy living – people get wrapped up in the technicalities of the disorder or the vagaries of the word "recovery" and use these things as ways to avoid actually doing the work involved in achieving the goal.

What will it take to recover?

Hard work. Scary moments. Brutal honesty. Self-love. Self-acceptance. Introspection. Patience.

> *"Patience with others is love. Patience with self is hope." ~ unknown*

Mostly it will take hard work, determination and perseverance to get off the roller coaster. If recovery were a cakewalk, there wouldn't be much BPD out in the world because everybody would just get in line to receive their dose of recovery and move on with their lives.

You'll need to keep in mind that the traits listed in the DSM-IV Diagnostic Criteria are things that you learned a long time ago, and have had years to practice to perfection. Your goal in recovery is to discard those old ways of doing things, learn new healthy ways and practice them until they become second-nature. It takes more than a week or a month to undo a lifetime of learning.

No one expects you to be able to wave a magic wand and miraculously become someone new overnight. Be sure that your expectations are reasonable and that you cut yourself some slack. You will not be perfect the first time you try a new technique. You may not even be adept with the technique after a hundred attempts or a year of practice. And the beautiful part is that no one expects you to be perfect or get it right the very first time.

There will be times when you'll stumble or backslide, and you'll want to beat yourself up – literally or figuratively. But if stumbling is discussed in this guide, doesn't it stand to reason that it's a normal part of the recovery process? You're not alone and you're not a failure. You'll need to learn to handle disappointments and setbacks because those are things that will never stop happening in life.

An analogy to the recovery process

We will explore the essence of Borderline a little further along in this guide, so rather than getting into some of the more specific aspects, we can stick to an analogy for now.

We're fragmented people. We have these different pieces and parts that make us who we are. If we imagine a broken mirror lying on the floor and we pick up one shard, that's all we see at that moment. There isn't a whole mirror. There isn't anything of value. There's just this tiny, useless, pathetic, broken shard that serves no purpose. And yet, when we look away from the broken bits on the floor and catch our reflection in a window, on the back of a spoon, see ourselves reflected back by someone we love, we feel euphoric, wonderful, on top of the world. Then we notice the broken bits on the floor and we're immediately plummeted back into the "reality of worthlessness. "Those voices that battle inside of us are the shards of mirror. We don't know how to imagine them coming together to form anything of value. We wouldn't even know where to begin because there are so many - it's worse than the worst jigsaw puzzle. Start with one piece at a time. Pick it up carefully, don't hurt yourself with it, look at it, maybe paint it pink or purple or blue or orange, maybe file the sharp edges down, maybe reshape it into a piece that might fit nicely with another piece. Recovery is your opportunity to recreate yourself however you'd like to be. You don't have to conform to anyone's ideas or expectations. You don't have to be who you've always been. You can become whoever and whatever you'd like. YOU have the power to create a beautiful mosaic mirror of yourself.

The possibility of medication(s)

Borderline is not necessarily a biological disorder. While there are believed to be some biological underpinnings or a hereditary predisposition toward BPD, there is no causal relationship established, nor are there any BPD meds, per se. Since BPD is generally co-morbid (found in conjunction with) other disorders, medications are generally prescribed that can treat the accompanying disorders, or control the symptoms to a functional level.

Because the road to recovery, especially in this guide, focuses on retraining actions, reactions and interactions with the world, it is essential that the appropriate medication or combination of medications are ascertained to best modulate the physiology, enabling us to focus on the work of recovery rather than be continually distracted by the roller coaster ride.

42   Putting The Pieces Together

Figure 3.1 is a visual representation of a sample Borderline's mood swings without medications to modulate the mood swings. Figure 3.2 is a visual representation of a sample Borderline's mood swings with mood stabilizing medication(s) under the same types of triggering situations.

Figure 3.1

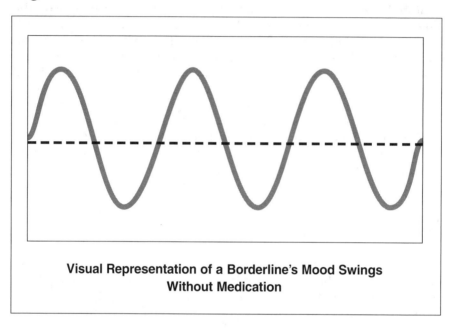

Visual Representation of a Borderline's Mood Swings Without Medication

Figure 3.2 is also indicative of a "normal" person's mood swings. The ups-and-downs in life are what make us human. Part of the key to recovery is determining what a healthy and reasonable mood swing feels like.

You may notice as well that Figure 3.1 has some dips below the baseline. These dips represent the intensity of feelings of worthlessness, suicidal idealism, self-injury and the other heart-pounding trips downward on the roller coaster of BPD.

In Figure 3.2 you will notice that those dips below the baseline simply do not exist. Sure, the healthy person's mood drops in accordance with certain situations, however a moderate dip is quite different from a plunge to the opposite end of the spectrum. This will be the goal of recovery – modulated and healthy emotional responses to ordinarily (for the world of Borderline) triggering situations.

Figure 3.2

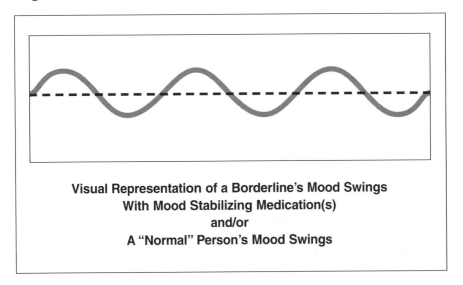

Visual Representation of a Borderline's Mood Swings
With Mood Stabilizing Medication(s)
and/or
A "Normal" Person's Mood Swings

The necessity of the support system

A support system is critical during recovery. Many Borderlines, when told they should have a support system, tell of how no one loves them, no one wants to be around them, no one cares about them at all, that they have no one in the world. This is patently untrue.

While it might feel true, it is most likely that the Borderlines perceptions have been skewed. Or that the Borderline is feeling such self-loathing that they find it impossible to admit that another person could possibly care about such a worthless creature as themselves. (Many Borderlines have perfected the martyr role due to thinking such as this.)

If perhaps you've burned a few bridges, been unusually harsh to friends and honestly believe you have no one for you in the world, then this is the perfect time to start building your support network. The mirror analogy discussed putting the bits and shards of yourself back together into a beautiful mirror mosaic that you can proudly call your own. In building the support network, you can begin with new faces, people who have no preconceived notions of you, who don't pre-judge you based on your past actions or indiscretions.

> *"The best part of not knowing who you are is the opportunity to become who you want."* ~ *Lisa Musing*

Just about anyone can be in a support system: close family members, significant others, dear friends, close colleagues, professional mentors, therapists, or online peers in support groups. These people don't necessarily need to know about the BPD (as is discussed in Chapter 12) but you should have a conscious awareness that you consider them to be part of your support system. By making this distinction for yourself, you're designating that person to be treated with deference or special attention. You've determined that you respect this person on a basic level enough to count on them in a time of crisis or uncertainty. You will be relying on these people in many, but often different and distinct, ways during the journey of recovery and healing.

The importance of honesty

Oftentimes we hear of people who see therapists and are unable to speak up, to say what's on their minds. This is not so much dishonesty as it is cheating oneself out of the value and reward of utilizing the wealth of resources available in the form of a trained, qualified, competent therapist. (More discussion about therapists in Chapter 4.)

- The most crucial time for honesty is when looking within. When we delude ourselves, when we lie to ourselves, when we look away because we have a feeling that looking within might be frightful or painful, we do ourselves a grave disservice, and truly defeat the concept of recovery. There are as many ways to go about recovery as there are people, and each person's journey toward recovery will be unique. However, some choose the psychoanalytic route which depends entirely on one's ability to look within, look to the past, face the events, feelings, traumas and be completely honest. (More discussion about types of therapy in Chapter 5.)

- Learning the value of speaking candidly about our feelings is also extremely important. Part of the recovery process is to learn to identify the swirling emotions within during those overwhelming periods so that they can be traced back to their origin. Determining the origin is important for working with most of the coping techniques – as discussed in Chapters 8 through 10. Being able to identify the emotion and then relate that emotion to someone within the support system is crucial to recovery.

Attention to detail

When we are on the roller coaster, we often feel overwhelmed. We have an emotional response to a trigger, and it feels like we are being crushed under a tidal wave of emotion. Oftentimes, we simply feel the raw emotion, and cannot differentiate between any subtle variations. Due to this inability to detect nuances and minor details, we have fostered a gut-level visceral reaction to anything overwhelming – usually a toss-up between rage and depression. Happiness doesn't usually enter the equation because things are black-and-white in the world of Borderline. Happiness isn't happiness; it's euphoria when we turn away from the broken shards of our own mirrors. But we have learned that the overwhelming emotions indicate "we did something wrong" (hence the rage and/or depression).

By learning to pay attention to the subtleties of emotional responses, by learning to backtrack to the point of origin in triggering situations, we will also be learning to see the grey in the world around us.

Many schools of thought suggest journaling as a way to bring out and examine these feelings and situations. This guide takes it to a more basic level: www.imood.com. This is a website that lists hundreds of moods from which one may choose at any given time. There are also small smiley (or not-so-smiley) faces that can be attached to the mood of the moment. Many internet websites, discussion boards or support groups will encourage their members to register for a free account to remind themselves and each other to keep track of how they're feeling at any given moment.

Homework

While these exercises may not seem like they're in-depth or very detailed, if you properly devote time to them and reach deep within yourself, you will yield great benefits. As the chapters go on, the exercises will become more detailed. For now, simply view this chapter's homework as another set of building blocks and do the best you can.

- Write about your feelings as you consider the possibility of your own recovery from BPD.

- Write about how you envision your life as a recovered Borderline.

- Identify members of your support system and give a brief description of their role in your life.

- Discuss past experiences (if any) you've had with medications, and explore your feelings about medications as part of your recovery.

4
Do I Need a Therapist?

While having a therapist in the support system during recovery work is suggested and could be highly advantageous, it is not necessarily a requirement. Nor is every therapist a benefit, as some can be detrimental to growth. And sometimes, due to the nature of Borderline, it can be difficult to distinguish whether the therapist is competent or if the Borderline is being hypersensitive.

I can't afford a therapist.

We have found that the mental health system in Canada is lacking in therapists, and that there is often a two year waiting list to get on the list to see a therapist for a twelve-session block. If you cannot afford a therapist or do not have access to one, there is still hope.

As mentioned in Chapter 3 when discussing the necessity of a support system, the therapist was one of many potential individuals in that group. Therapists are indeed helpful to have around, however they are not mandatory. It's not as though the therapist does all the work for you. The hard work is done within oneself and takes a great deal of dedication, determination and practice with coping techniques and honesty during introspection.

Many therapists will work on a sliding scale fee program. This means that they will adjust their rates to accommodate your economic situation. This does not mean that they will see you for ten dollars per session if their fee is normally $180.00 per hour. It means that they will work to get you the help you need.

You should also check with your local, county and state programs. Oftentimes, the county provides mental health services, usually in the form of social workers. These services may be free or very inexpensive, and it doesn't hurt to check around.

If you are paying for your therapy sessions out of your own pocket without insurance coverage, you should work with the therapist to set the schedule in the most effective and efficient manner possible. While it might be ideal to see the therapist three times a week, you may only be able to afford twice a month. Work with your therapist and ask for suggestions on how to cope during the time between sessions. Maybe your therapist will give you homework, much like this guide, or maybe he or she will be able to give you some resources you hadn't heard of before.

Appendices B and C contain Support Networks and Resources available for those who will be working on their recovery without the involvement of a therapist.

What kind of therapist should I find?

First and foremost, find a therapist you feel comfortable with. You should have a general, basic rapport with the person who will be asking you intimate questions and to whom you will be baring your soul. This is the person who will be your primary coach and will see you at probably some of the worst times in your recovery.

Many people will schedule an initial consultation with a prospective new therapist to get to know them, find out about their treatment style, get to see the therapist's office, discuss the therapist's educational background. Some people pick a therapist at random or place a slew of phone calls and end up with the first therapist who calls back.

A word of caution: you do not need to be best friends with this person. They are not your parent. They are not your sibling. They are not your childhood friend. If they are a competent therapist, you will know nothing about them personally. You won't know their family life, their upbringing, or their political or religious views. They will be a blank screen for you.

Many times people express a fear that the therapist is in a position of power, and they are perhaps afraid of or intimidated by the therapist. We encourage you to take the therapists off the pedestals. They know how the mind works just as a car mechanic or computer programmer knows how to fix your transmission or computer and yet we are rarely afraid of our mechanics or our tech support personnel. They simply have a different area of expertise.

They are not gods. They should not be worshiped, adored or fallen in love with. They should be respected and treated professionally.

You are, of course, entitled to ask the therapist credibility questions such as:

- Where did they go to school?
- What degrees do they have?
- What further education have they received since graduation?
- What experience do they have with BPD?
- What success rates do they personally have with BPD patients?
- How many cases per year, or what percentage of BPD patients do they treat?
- What methodology do they use in treating BPD?
- What do they believe causes BPD?

Handling crisis

There are invariably times of crisis between sessions. Times when the world seems to be falling apart, and when you don't feel able to go on any longer. Your therapist will probably give you a pager number or the number to his or her answering service, and will probably tell you that you can call at any time. They may even give you their email information.

Crisis is crisis is crisis. There are times when you feel an overwhelming need to speak with your therapist. Again, though, the therapist is a person. They should not be expected to be at your beck-and-call twenty-four hours a day, seven days a week. They should not receive nightly or even weekly crisis telephone calls. They should not receive eighteen emails a week describing in excruciating detail all the things you're feeling at each particular moment. They should be respected as the professionals they are.

A goal of therapy should be self-sufficiency, and while the therapist will be open to an emergency call now and then during the first portions of therapy – say, the first six months – it's probably best if you and your therapist work together to find alternative ways for you to handle crisis without involving the therapist.

Borderlines are allowed to have crisis feelings and emergencies, and they should be comfortable enough to know that their therapist is there for them in a pinch. However, there is a difference between leaning on the therapist (or anyone else) for occasional support and becoming utterly dependent upon the therapist (or anyone else) and being unable to function without that person always available.

It's a good idea to discuss these things with your therapist early on in the relationship or even bring them up in the initial consultation to see how that particular therapist handles crisis situations. If you're expecting that they will call you back immediately, and they have a policy in which they wait one full hour before returning calls, you may be pretty rattled the first time you have a crisis and your expectations are dashed.

What if I don't like the therapist I find or the one I already have?

There is no law that says you are obligated to continue seeing a therapist you're uncomfortable with – unless, of course, you're under some sort of court-ordered counseling or sanctions.

When initially selecting a therapist, you may wish to ask the receptionist or office manager some of the basic questions to determine if you feel there would be a good match to suit your needs and/or comfort level. Beyond that, it may be a wise idea to either schedule a preliminary meeting with the therapist to meet with him or her face to face, or ask to speak with the therapist over the phone to save time and a trip and possibly some money.

If you've already scheduled an appointment with a therapist you don't want to return to see, please make sure you phone the receptionist to cancel. Many a Borderline has resorted to the ostrich method of sticking their head in the sand, and ended up with some cancellation charges following them around. If you can't do it by phone for fear of being grilled, intimidated or chickening out, send a letter or a fax. Use your head, be smart and save your money for a therapist you do feel comfortable with.

Is it me or is it the therapist?

It's not uncommon for the therapist and patient to clash for whatever reason. What makes things difficult for someone with

Borderline is determining where the boundaries are. Is it that the therapist is wacky and totally incompetent? Or is the Borderline being hypersensitive? Has the therapist been split? Did the Borderline put the therapist on a pedestal from which they've fallen? Has transference occurred, the process by which the therapist remains a blank slate for the patient to pour all feelings about past incidences, thereby absorbing the brunt of the emotional response to the past?

It can be a very fine line. Not all Borderlines will split their therapists. Not all Borderlines will engage in transference. Not all therapists are competent and qualified to handle BPD cases. There are some therapists who refuse to take any BPD patients, some who will only take a specific number of BPD patients and some who've not even encountered BPD before.

There are some coping techniques which will be discussed later in this guide to help the Borderline figure out how to make a healthy decision about an uncomfortable therapy situation.

Where can I find a therapist?

There are many places to obtain the names of therapists:

- The Resources section of this guide lists several therapist locator websites.

- Your company's health insurance plan may offer a separate and confidential mental health program benefit.

- Your company may offer an Employee Assistance program.

- Online support groups may be able to provide you with a local referral.

- Your county health department may be able to direct you toward some local resources.

- The Yellow Pages telephone directory may get you started with therapist names.

How long will recovery take?

Again, this question is only answerable by the individual embarking upon the journey toward recovery because, like snowflakes, we are all unique individuals with our own level of determination, drive, ability to stand back up and brush the dust off and ability to practice, learn, heal and grow.

There is no set time period for recovery. This is not like the Cabbage Soup Diet which promises losing 12 pounds in two weeks. The process of recovery truly is dependent upon the work you do, the effort you invest and the willingness to fight for your own mental health.

Generally, improvements can be seen within a few months and lifestyle changes show themselves within the first year. Once the behavioral aspects are addressed and coping techniques are learned, the Borderline is better able to handle him or herself outwardly. However, there will probably still be some underlying issues and uncertainties. These things may take another year, two years or five years to work through.

The point is that simply reading a book or seeing a therapist once a week won't make the changes happen instantly. Be prepared for months and years of work to overcome and undo decades of learned behavior.

Couch Potato to Olympic Decathlon

Imagine that we look into John's life and we see him laying on the sofa, grossly overweight, wearing a stained and torn undershirt and boxer briefs, eating corn chips by the handful with the remote control in the other hand. John doesn't get off the couch a whole lot, other than to get his next snack. He doesn't pay any attention to his appearance. He doesn't go out of his way to make an effort at much of anything beyond the remote control.

One day, John flips the channel and sees a telecast of the Olympic Decathlon and becomes inspired. John gets up off the couch, steps outside (without changing his clothes) and tries to complete a decathlon.

What do you think the results of John's first attempt at being a competitor in the Decathlon are?

Like John, most Borderlines who begin the journey to recovery have a misguided notion that simply because they've read the coping techniques (or watched the Olympics) that they're "good to go" and because they believe in themselves (without basis in reality or historical data to back up their beliefs), they can accomplish anything they set their mind to.

Unfortunately, life isn't that simple. If it were, we'd all be world-class athletes, financial wizards, real estate tycoons and Recovered Borderlines.

John isn't able to become an Olympic Decathlete simply by sheer force of will. He needs to train. He needs a coach. He needs to practice every single day and push himself to the limits. He needs to try new things. He needs to get off his duff and build up a sweat.

Likewise, with recovery, you are not expected to run a marathon or swim ten miles in open water simply because you now know that recovery is possible. It will take time and practice. You will have to learn new concepts, listen to your coach and challenge yourself.

The direct effect of input on recovery output

There's an old computer acronym: WYSIWYG (wizzy-wig) that stands for "What you see is what you get." It means that what you get out of the system is only as good as what you put into the system. The same holds true for recovery. If you don't put the effort, practice and honesty into recovery, you won't get the full effects.

How long your recovery takes is entirely dependent upon one person: YOU.

It's challenging; it's tough; it's heart-wrenching; it's frustrating; it's aggravating; it can feel like it's an insurmountable challenge.

It is totally worth every ounce of effort put in on the front-end.

Don't expect to be "cured" within a couple of weeks. Don't expect to be "normal" after a couple of therapy sessions. Don't expect to be "all better" after a couple of months.

It took years, even decades, perhaps even an entire lifetime, to learn and hone the Borderline behaviors into the cruel art that they are. That cannot be undone overnight.

Why does it feel like therapy makes me/my life worse instead of better?

If you can imagine a serene and quiet pond, one that's been undisturbed for a long time – no children swimming in it, no storms swirling above it, no boats racing across it. Then imagine a tornado coming through the area and getting very close to the pond. The force of nature will undoubtedly stir up the sediment that has spent months or years lying peacefully at the bottom, and once the storm passes, the pond no longer looks like it once did. t now looks dingy and clouded with the stirred up sediment.

The pond still holds the same water and same sediment but it looks different now. Maybe it looks less appealing if you were interested in going for a swim, but it is still the same pond. It will take time for all the pond's components to settle back into place, a new place, design and orientation.

Therapy isn't easy – and if it is, it's probably a pretty good bet that you're not making much progress. Therapy is hard work and very draining. For me, personally, I was pleased with going every other week for the majority of my time in therapy because it gave me an opportunity to recover from the last session and re-integrate (in a more healthy way) the issues I'd dredged up. I was allowed the time to let the sediment in my pond resettle.

Homework

As you've been asked to focus on therapy and finding a therapist in this chapter, you're now asked to explore your feelings and thoughts about therapy.

- Write about what you're looking for in a therapist. What would make you feel comfortable? Does their gender matter to you?
- Write about what you expect to get out of therapy and what you expect from your therapist.
- Write about your past experiences with therapy. Did you gain insights, make progress, learn about yourself? How did past therapists handle your volatile personality?
- Discuss the past experiences (if any) you've had with medications, and explore your feelings about medications as part of your recovery.

Therapeutic Approaches

That recovery is entirely unique to the person recovering cannot be stressed enough. What makes sense to one person with Borderline may not make sense at all to someone else. Likewise, the way in which a person approaches their therapy is also unique. Anyone who says that their way is best, or the only true way to recover from BPD is a victim of the black-and-white thinking discussed earlier in this guide.

Cognitive Behavior Therapy – CBT

Cognitive behavior therapy combines two very effective kinds of psychotherapy — cognitive therapy and behavior therapy.

Behavior therapy helps you weaken the *connections* between troublesome situations and your habitual reactions— such as fear, depression or rage, and self-defeating or self-damaging behavior—to them. It also teaches you how to calm your mind and body, so you can feel better, think more clearly and make better decisions.

Cognitive therapy teaches you how certain *thinking patterns* are causing your symptoms — by giving you a distorted picture of what's going on in your life, and making you feel anxious, depressed or angry for no good reason, or provoking you into ill-chosen actions.

When combined into CBT, behavior therapy and cognitive therapy provide you with very powerful tools for stopping your symptoms, and getting your life on a more satisfying track.

In CBT your therapist takes an active part in solving your problems. He or she doesn't settle for just nodding wisely while you carry the whole burden of finding the answers. You will receive a thorough diagnostic workup at the beginning of treatment — to make sure your needs and problems have been pinpointed as well as possible.

56   Putting The Pieces Together

This crucial step — which is often skimped or omitted altogether in traditional kinds of therapy — results in an explicit, understandable and flexible treatment plan that accurately reflects your own individual needs. In many ways CBT resembles education, coaching or tutoring. Under expert guidance, as a CBT client you will share in setting treatment goals, and in deciding which techniques work best for you personally.

CBT provides clear structure and focus on treatment. Unlike therapies that easily drift off into interesting but unproductive side trips, CBT sticks to the point and changes course only when there are sound reasons for doing so.

As a participant in CBT, you will take on valuable "homework" assignments to speed your progress. These tasks — which are developed as much as possible with your own active participation — extend and multiply the results of the work done in your therapist's office. You may also receive take-home readings and other materials tailored to your own individual needs to help you continue to forge ahead between sessions.

Most people coming for therapy need to change something in their lives — whether it's the way they feel, the way they act, or how other people treat them. CBT focuses on finding out just what needs to be changed and what doesn't — and then works for those targeted changes. Some exploration of people's life histories is necessary and desirable — if their current problems are closely tied to "unfinished emotional business" from the past, or if they grow out of a repeating pattern of difficulty. Nevertheless, 100 years of psychotherapy has made this clear:

Focusing on the past (and on dreams) can at times help *explain* a person's difficulties. But these activities all too often do little to actually *overcome* them. Instead, in CBT we aim at rapid improvement in your feelings and moods, and early changes in any self-defeating behavior you may be caught up in. As you can see, CBT is more present-centered and forward-looking than traditional therapies.

The two most powerful levers of constructive change (apart from medication) are the following:

Altering ways of thinking — a person's thoughts, beliefs, ideas, attitudes, assumptions, mental imagery, and ways of directing his or her attention — for the better. This is the *cognitive* aspect of CBT.

Helping a person greet the challenges and opportunities in his or her life with a clear and calm mind — and then taking actions that are likely to have desirable results. This is the *behavioral* aspect of CBT.

In other words, CBT focuses on exactly what traditional therapies tend to leave out — how to achieve *beneficial change*, as opposed to mere explanation or "insight."

CBT has been very thoroughly researched. In study after study, it has proven to be as effective as drugs in treating both depression and anxiety.

In particular, CBT has proven to be *better* than drugs in avoiding treatment failures, and in preventing relapse after the end of treatment. If you are concerned about your ability to complete treatment and maintain your gains thereafter, keep this in mind.

Other symptoms for which CBT has demonstrated its effectiveness include problems with relationships, family, work, school, insomnia, and self-esteem. And it is usually the *preferred* treatment for shyness, headaches, panic attacks, phobias, post-traumatic stress, eating disorders, loneliness, and procrastination. It can also be combined, if needed, with psychiatric medications.[3]

Dialectical Behavior Therapy – DBT

Marsha Linehan, Ph.D. (1991) pioneered this treatment, based on the idea that psychosocial treatment of those with BPD was as important in controlling the condition as traditional psycho- and pharmacotherapy were. Concomitant with this belief was a hierarchical structure of treatment goals. Paramount among these was reducing parasuicidal (self-injuring) and life-threatening behaviors. Next came reducing behaviors that interfered with the therapy/treatment process, and finally reducing behaviors that reduced the client's quality of life. In 1991, Linehan published results of a study that does remarkably well at achieving these goals.

The Theory

Basically, DBT maintains that some people, due to invalidating environments during upbringing, and due to biological factors as yet unknown, react abnormally to emotional stimulation. Their level of arousal goes up much more quickly, peaks at a higher level, and takes more time to return to baseline. This explains why borderlines are known for crisis-strewn lives and extreme emotional liability (emotions that shift rapidly). Because of their past invalidation, they don't have any methods for coping with these sudden, intense surges of emotion. DBT is a method for teaching skills that will help in this task.

How it works

Dialectical Behavioral Therapy (DBT) consists of two parts:

Part I: Once-weekly, psychotherapy sessions in which a particular problematic behavior or event from the past week is explored in detail, beginning with the chain of events leading up to it, going through alternative solutions that might have been used and examining what kept the client from using more adaptive solutions to the problem.

Both between and during sessions, the therapist actively teaches and reinforces adaptive behaviors, especially as they occur within the therapeutic relationship. The emphasis is on teaching patients how to manage emotional trauma rather than reducing or taking them out of crises. Telephone contact with the individual therapist between sessions is part of DBT procedures (Linehan, 1991).

DBT targets behaviors in a descending hierarchy:

- decreasing high-risk suicidal behaviors
- decreasing responses or behaviors (by either therapist or patient) that interfere with therapy
- decreasing behaviors that interfere with/reduce quality of life
- decreasing and dealing with post-traumatic stress responses
- enhancing respect for self
- acquisition of the behavioral skills taught in group
- additional goals set by patient

Part II: Weekly 2.5-hour group therapy sessions in which interpersonal effectiveness, distress tolerance/reality acceptance skills, emotion regulation, and mindfulness skills are taught. Group therapists are not available over the phone between sessions; they refer patients in crisis to the individual therapist.[4]

Psychoanalysis

Many people swear by psychoanalysis and confronting their pasts, coming to terms with old issues and dealing with old feelings that continue to haunt them years, even decades, later.

Psychoanalysis is oftentimes a grueling process wherein the patient establishes a safe relationship with the therapist before beginning to explore incidents in their past, often reliving the exact emotional turmoil and psychological trauma of the moment.

The results or effects of psychoanalysis generally take a longer period of time to develop because there is usually a lot of history to be worked through. In the behavior therapy approaches, the results are a little more immediate because the Borderline is given adult coping mechanisms and trained in new ways to deal with the outside world, thus achieving more harmonious results.

Those who have undergone the psychoanalytic route often praise its ability to address the inner feelings rather than simply controlling the outward actions. They claim that to mask the inner self that has been present from birth, through infancy and childhood, by creating new structures of acceptable actions, the Borderline may be only doing part of the work necessary for true recovery.

In other words, it's one thing to know that you have an urge to scream and yell because you got onion rings instead of the French fries you ordered, and another to be mature enough to control that impulse and politely ask the server to correct the mistake.

Those who believe in the psychoanalytic approach would point out that the desire to scream and yell stem possibly from feelings of worthlessness obtained during childhood during a situation with a parent, caregiver, sibling or playmate who told you that you weren't good enough to get the last order of French fries, and you should just be happy with the onion rings because you don't even deserve those.

The psychoanalytic approach is more likely to address the moment in time when the feelings first became prevalent, and "make peace" with the past situation by identifying and coping with those feelings.

Self-help and peer support

As was briefly mentioned in the discussion about finding a therapist, it is possible to make remarkable progress "on your own" – that is to say, without a formal therapist or therapy program like CBT. We are never truly on our own because, as the saying goes, "no man is an island."

Self-help and peer support have their own sub-heading in this chapter even though they've already been discussed. The peer support is basically the support system which is crucial to recovery and was discussed in Chapter 3. The self-help is the hard work a Borderline needs to do in order to get themselves healthier and happier, as was also discussed in Chapter 3.

Self-help can get tricky and downright scary unless you have a solid support network in place. A support network can include any combination of the following:

- friends
- family (siblings, parents, extended family)
- co-workers
- romantic partners
- internet friends/peers
- formal support groups (with regular meetings, possibly with sponsors or buddies)

The last thing you should ever feel is that you're alone as you go through some of the tougher aspects of recovery from Borderline. This doesn't mean that you should expect those in your support network to fully understand what you're going through, thinking or feeling, but that you should always have a shoulder you can cry on. It means that you have a couple of sounding boards, people to bounce things off of when you're unsure whether or not you're overreacting or making a good decision, etc.

In case I haven't made it perfectly clear, let me say one more time in no uncertain terms: you should have a solid support network. How many people make up a network? The answer depends you and your needs, for sure, but **the only truly wrong answer** is "a network can be one person." If you attempt to rely on a single person to support you, you're setting yourself up for failure. If you ask a man to carry an elephant on his back, he would be crushed under the weight. If you ask a hundred men to carry an elephant, they would be successful because each was only supporting a fraction of the elephant's bulk. Similarly, the more people you have in your support network, the more likely you are to be successful.

So who should be in your support network? That's entirely up to you. I recommend you take a look at some of the types of situations you know trigger you into a downward BPD spiral. Categorize them. Perhaps you need help in dealing with workplace stress. Perhaps you would like some assistance getting through interactions with your mother. Perhaps you need to figure out how to deal with minor disappointments when friends flake out on you or change plans at the last moment.

Once you've identified the areas in which you think you might be able to improve, start to take a look around you and figure out who you admire and/or respect for those specific things. Maybe you've noticed that Megan remains cool under fire at work, never gets flustered and always handles situations with unflappable calm no matter what. Maybe you realize that Amy is more easy-going than you, doesn't get all bent out of shape when plans change and is able to express displeasure to her friends without losing them. Maybe you see that Julie doesn't let her mother get to her, no matter how nasty or acerbic the woman is; Julie just lets those snippy, sarcastic comments slide on by without so much as a blip in the blood pressure.

Megan, Amy and Julie should certainly be added to your support network.

Homework

We have covered a lot of ground in this section. These exercises are to help you examine the various choices available to you as you proceed toward recovery.

- Take about twenty minutes to reflect on each of the topics covered in this section:

    – Cognitive Behavior Therapy

    – Dialectic Behavior Therapy

62 Putting The Pieces Together

- Psychoanalysis

- Self-Help with Peer Support

- Which one of these therapeutic approaches resonated most with you? Did one stand out over the others? Why do you think that is?

- If financial considerations and access to care were not issues for you, what do you envision would happen during your journey through the therapeutic approach that most appeals to you?

- If you are hampered by finances and/or access to care, how do you propose to work around these challenges to obtain the recovery you deserve?

- How long do you believe recovery would (or should) take, in general? For you? With the therapeutic option of your choice? With some other course toward recovery?

6
Do I Need Medication?

Medication has long been a sore spot for many individuals who have been in-and-out of the mental health system. Many people react strongly against being a guinea pig for a mad scientist to "play chemistry set" while disrupting their lives, their ability to function and in some cases make things worse.

Meds are likely to help

Most often, Borderlines will have a psychiatrist who will be the one prescribing and adjusting the medications, and they will also have a therapist. The psychiatrist has the ability to prescribe medication; however, there should be a dialogue between the therapist and the psychiatrist to ensure that the psychiatrist is getting a full and accurate picture of the effects of the medications.

There are many Borderlines who've been overmedicated in the past, and have determined that since their problems are mental, they can overcome the problems by sheer force of will. This is generally not a likely scenario. As was pointed out in the example of the Couch Potato, simply knowing where the problem is doesn't make the "cure" happen miraculously.

Because BPD has been difficult to diagnose in the past due to the high occurrence of co-morbidity and the patient's ability to display many different symptoms or only display portions of their actual symptom repertoire, psychiatrists have had a rough time getting the medications to balance at an acceptable plateau. Many patients have complained of losing creativity, feeling like a zombie, being inordinately sleepy, losing concentration. Sometimes it seems like the side effects are worse than the disorder they're trying to alleviate.

While recovery from BPD is generally handled through perception modification either through DBT, CBT or psychoanalysis, in order to allow the Borderline to be able to do the work necessary to get themselves into a healthier state of mind, it is most likely that a mood stabilization medication needs to be introduced. Again, BPD is often presented in conjunction with so many different disorders such as ADHD (Attention Deficit with Hyperactivity Disorder), OCD (Obsessive Compulsive Disorder), Bi-Polar, GAD (Generalized Anxiety Disorder), SAD (Seasonal Affective Disorder), PTSD (Post Traumatic Stress Disorder) and many others.

The main goal of medication therapy is not to "cure" the BPD, nor is it to squash all shreds of humanity and turn the patient into a drooling lump. The main goal of medication therapy is to even out the mood swings. Some additional goals might be to control the paranoia, calm the racing thoughts, reduce the sky-high anxiety or basically address the major hurdles to ordinary thinking that are created through the co-morbid disorders.

The most common medications prescribed are either antidepressants or anti-anxiety drugs. These generally have the layperson's usage of the term "mood stabilization," while they're not technically classified as mood stabilizers. The medications should serve to calm the thinking, even out the mood swings and/or lift the mood so that the Borderline is able to figuratively lift their head high, and focus long enough on doing the work that needs to be done to train for the Olympic Decathlon.

What classes of medications are there?

Table 4.1 Table of Antidepressants

Antidepressant Drug Class	Chemical Name (and Trade Name)*
Tricyclic Antidepressants – three linked molecular rings.	Amitriptyline (Elavil, Endep) Clomipramine (Anafranil) Desipramine (Norapramin, Pertofrane) Doxepin (Adapin, Sinequan) Imipramine (Tofranil) Nortiptyline (Aventyl) Protriptyline (Vivactil) Trimipramine (Surmontil)
Tetracyclic Antidepressants – four linked molecular rings.	Amoxapine (Asendin) Maprotiline (Ludiomil)
SSRI Antidepressants – selective serotonin reuptake inhibitors which have selective effects on nerves that use serotonin as a transmitter substance.	Citalopram (Celexa) Fluoxetine (Prozac) Fluvoxamine (Luvox) Paroxetine (Paxil) Sertraline (Zoloft)
MAO Inhibitors – prevents breakdown of chemical messengers like serotonin, norepinephrine and dopamine within the nerves.	Isocarboxazid (Marplan) Phenelzine (Nardil) Selegiline (Eldepryl) Tranylcypromine (Parnate)
Serotonin Antagonists – boosts serotonin levels within the body by blocking its reuptake at nerve synapses, much like the SSRIs however these drugs have less potent effects on the serotonin pump than the SSRIs or even the older tricyclic antidepressants.	Nefazodone (Serzone) Trazodone (Desyrel)
Other Antidepressants	Bupropion (Wellbutrin) Mirtazapine (Remeron) Venlafaxine (Effexor)
Mood Stabilizers	Carbamazepine (Tegretol) Gabapentin (Neurontin) Lamotrigine (Lamictal) Lithium (Eskalith) Valproic Acid (Depakene) Dicalproex Sodium (Depakote)

Table 4.2 – Table of Anti-Anxiety Medications

Anti-Anxiety Drug Class	Chemical Name (and Trade Name)*
Benxodiazepines (minor tranquilizers)	Alprazolam (Xanax) Chlordiazepoxide (Librium) Clonazepam (Klonopin) Clorazepate (Tranxene, Tranxene-SD) Diazepam (Valium) Halazepam (Paxipam) Lorazepam (Ativan) Oxazepam (Serax) Prazepam (Centrax – discontinued)
Other Anti-Anxiety Drugs	Buspirone (BuSpar) Meprobamate (Equanil, Miltown)
Antihistimines	Diphenhydramine (Benadryl) Hroxyzine Pamoate (Vistaril)
Beta-Blocking Agents	Atenolol (Tenormin) Nadolol (Corgard) Propranolol (Inderal)
Alpha-Agonists	Clonidine (Catapres)

Homework

Many people have different thoughts, feelings and reactions to being prescribed medication(s) for their mental well-being. These exercises are to help you get in touch with what's going on inside of yourself as you face the possibility or reality of such a situation.

- Write about your hopes and fears of being on medication.

- Write about your past experiences with medications. How did you feel? Did you have any strong emotional or psychological reactions? Physical reactions?

- Write about how you feel about the possibility of being on a medication for many years. The possibility of being on medication for rest of your life.

- Write about what side effects you would consider tolerable. What side effects you would not be able to tolerate.

Mirroring

Mirroring is one of those words that can mean so many different things depending on the situation and subject matter. In this chapter, we will discuss some of the different mirroring methods and their pros and cons.

The Chameleon

When someone doesn't have a clear sense of self, they will often times try to blend in with their surroundings. They'll be the consummate professional at work; the jock with a bunch of guys; the prissy female with a group of high society women; a seductress at the bar.

There are plenty of times when healthy people are called upon to accentuate different aspects of their personality. It would, of course, be unwise to be the seductress in a national sales meeting. Likewise, it would be very awkward to be the jock in a high society luncheon. We're all called on to wear different hats and show different aspects of ourselves in different social settings, however, when we don't have a strong sense of self, what we're doing is different from putting on a different hat. We're changing the costume entirely.

One of the key goals to recovery is to determine what the basic wardrobe is, and then learn that it's okay to wear the different hats or accessories depending on the situation at hand. This can be a very confusing concept to understand. We'll try to work through that murkiness together in this guide.

Mirroring as Reflection of Others

There are plenty of texts and resources that use the term "mirroring" to convey a very specific type of behavior. In their use of the term, they mean to imply that when a person with a very weak or limited sense of self finds someone they like, respect, or admire (or even loathe, despise or hate), that person will mirror the other person's words, professed beliefs and actions. Mirroring is similar to the chameleon aspect we just discussed but also slightly different.

In the chameleon role, the individual assumes the characteristics of their surroundings to blend in and be accepted. In this version of mirroring, we see the individual reflecting back the other person's words or actions and believing them to be their own words, professed beliefs or actions.

If you've ever lived in Texas (or even stayed there for an extended period of time) you may notice your Texas drawl come back when you're with or speaking to others who have the Texas drawl. An accent is one of the easiest things for most people to mirror. When it's put in front of us, we mirror it right back.

Being a chameleon entails shifting the portion of ourselves we choose to share with the world dependent upon the given social situation. Parroting or mirroring back the most noticeable characteristics of an individual in front of us at any given time is mirroring as a reflection of others.

Mirroring as Viewing Ourselves

There is a metaphysical belief that discusses mirroring human behavior. It's very different from the mirroring as reflection of others as just discussed. In this belief, when we respond to someone strongly with either love or loathing, we are really responding to the inner characteristics of ourselves.

Yes, this can be a bit confusing, but we'll take it slowly and give some examples of this type of mirroring.

Have you ever encountered someone who rubbed you the wrong way immediately? You weren't quite able to put your finger on it but you were just filled with anger or bitterness any time this person was around you? I think we have all experienced people like that. I think it is part of human nature, and is a perfectly natural experience.

Mirroring

As you think about one person you reacted too strongly in a negative way, how awful this person was, how rotten, how you would have done anything to get away from that person and never be exposed to them again, you're probably thinking this guide is full of horse hockey for even suggesting that the despised person was really a reflection of yourself!

Hold onto those horses for just a minute. This will be one of the tougher concepts you'll be asked to focus on in this guide. It may in fact be a concept that you'll blow past right now and come back to in a while – a week, six months, a year. You are not being asked to accept this concept. You are not being asked to believe this concept. You are not being asked to be a staunch supporter of this concept.

This mirroring concept is brought to your attention for the purpose of helping you discover your genuine self more clearly and possibly more quickly. This mirroring concept, if you can accept it even tentatively, will assist you in your recovery process a great deal.

Author notes:

When I first heard this metaphysical mirroring concept, it was in relation to this individual online who I just totally clashed with. I hated him. He was pompous, arrogant, conceited, self-centered, self-righteous and very condescending. I was livid at the person who suggested this belief to me! How dare they compare me to this bombastic fool! Can't they see that I'm a much nicer person than he is?!

As I allowed the belief to float around the back of my brain for a little while, as I continued to be very miffed at the whole idea, I thought about the guy I despised. I watched him a little more closely. I consciously compared his words and actions with my own.

And then it hit me. What I was reacting to in his words and actions were the stuff I didn't like in myself. I saw everything I hated about myself in this guy and it made me furious.

The person who shared the belief with me was right on target. Thanks Gator!

Conversely, the same is true in strong feelings of love and admiration. When we react to someone very intensely, the odds are pretty good that the things that attract us to that person so strongly and quickly are the things (aspects, characteristics, traits, qualities) that we want more of for ourselves. When we fall in love with someone, the initial attraction is usually to the things they bring to the table that we don't believe we have, or that we wish we had more of.

- "I wish I were as funny as him."
- "I wish I were as smart as her."
- "I love his sense of humor."
- "She's very analytical."
- "She's not nearly as emotional as I am."
- "He's so well-respected."

These are just a few examples of things that people say when they first meet and like someone a lot. And when we say or think things like this, the mirroring concept of this section says that we are attracted to those qualities or traits because they are things that we wish were stronger aspects of our own personalities. We invite these people into our lives so that we can bask in their limelight, absorb some of those tendencies and make them our own.

How is this different from being a chameleon or imitating the person as described in mirroring as a reflection of others? It's not so different, really. What makes this mirroring concept different from the first and most commonly accepted is that it applies to both types of strong reaction – love and loathing – and the emphasis is on the quest for the definition of the genuine self.

Perception

Perception is a very tricky and sticky topic. If you have psychotic breaks with reality or have experienced schizophrenia where entire people, relationships and situations were present, this is probably not a helpful section for you because it deals very much with the greyness of reality. If you already have or are currently experiencing a difficult time telling reality from psychotic episodes, I ask that you please discuss these things with your therapist and/or psychiatrist for appropriate medication and counseling.

How we perceive things around us – sights, sounds, smells, sensations – is part of who we are. Some of us have excellent eyesight with a keen sense of subtle color variations whereas others of us have "sniffers" that would command high salaries at major perfume houses. We're all unique in our individuality and that's a normal, wonderful thing.

We're not discussing perception of the substantive things of the world, such as the color of the sunset at the beach in Hawaii, nor are we discussing the relative hardness of various types of wood. Most of these things are relatively concrete and shared by all of humanity. This discussion will be based on the assumption that you're not having trouble determining fantasy or delusion from reality.

The perception we'll deal with in this section relates to interpersonal relationships. We've discussed the black-and-white thinking, and we know that one of the key goals of recovery is to learn to find the grey in the world. As part of the recovery process, you'll be asked to alter your perceptions, especially in interpersonal relationships.

There is power in thought. A metaphysical saying goes: "Thoughts are things." Thoughts and how we perceive things is a very crucial element to how we respond to those around us, and how deeply we allow our emotional state to be impacted. In this section, as we discuss perceptions, we'll be focusing on converting from black-and-white thinking and perception to grey thinking and perception.

Example #1 – Borderline Perception:

Amy: "That's a really interesting sweater. Where'd you get it?"

Borderline perception: Wow. 'Interesting.' She said 'interesting.' That must mean she couldn't think of anything nice to say about it. I must look like a complete dork or something. That was pretty rude of her. I mean, couldn't she say something at least nice, commented on the color or the weave? What a little snot!

Borderline reaction: "Like you really want to know! Get lost."

The perception is what shaped the response. The perception was skewed and based on a wide variety of assumptions – that "interesting" wasn't meant as a compliment, that Amy was being rude, that the Borderline's appearance was sub-standard.

The same comment from Amy with an altered perception results in a very different response.

> ### Example #1 – Altered Perception:
>
> Amy: "That's a really interesting sweater. Where did you get it?"
>
> Healthy perception: Amy finds the sweater interesting and wants to know where I got it. I wonder why she wants to know – maybe she wants to get a similar one or maybe she thinks it's downright hideous.
>
> Healthy response: "It is rather interesting, isn't it? I got it at ABC Clothing Store. Why do you ask?"

In this example, nothing is assumed and Amy's comments were taken at face value. While there was some confusion about the word "interesting" rather than making a negative assumption about the word, neutral clarification was sought.

It's a whole lot easier to jump to the conclusion of negativity and that's probably all you've known for most of your life. It's a very difficult habit to break, however, it is possible as part of recovery. Later in this guide, we'll focus on practical ways to get from the Borderline Perception to the Altered Perception.

Also, please note that I purposely used the terms "Borderline reaction" and "healthy response." There is a vital difference between a response and a reaction. The reaction always comes first and it is a visceral thing—the direct result of stimuli to our system. While two people may have the same reaction – such as "He's being a complete snot" – the healthy individual will have a different response than a Borderline response. The healthy individual will process the internal reaction, separate the stuff, examine the options available, choose the best one for the moment and act upon it. This usually results in a healthy response, as indicated in the above example. The Borderline individual will not take those steps to process the internal reaction, and may actually come right out and say, "Wow, you're being a complete snot!"

Perception plays a key role in our interpersonal relationships. If we are able to process our internal reactions and separate the stuff involved, our perception will likely shift of its own accord and thus make us more healthy individuals.

Homework

These exercises are to help you examine the various choices available to you as you proceed toward recovery.

- Pick one of the main topics we covered in this section that best describes you:

    – The Chameleon

    – Mirroring as a Reflection of Others

    – Mirroring as Viewing Ourselves

    – Perception

- Does this aspect of your self help you in daily life? Does it hinder you? In what ways?

- Reflect on or write about times in your life when you now recognize that you may have been mirroring, in any of the different versions.

- Based on what you've read in this section, what could you do differently to be healthier in your daily activities? Write out an action plan to achieve that goal.

- Reflect on or write about people in your experience who have used one of these techniques to their advantage. How did it help them? Do you think it was a healthy and appropriate use of that particular mirroring technique?

74   Putting The Pieces Together

The Four Agreements

A very wise man by the name of Don Miguel Ruiz has authored a book called "The Four Agreements." If you have not yet read this book, I strongly encourage you to pick up a copy at your local bookstore and spend some time with the material he presents.

I'd like to share with you the four basic agreements Mr. Ruiz discusses in his book, and then give you my own perception of the basic understandings and how they relate to recovering from BPD.

1. Be impeccable with your word.

2. Don't take anything personally.

3. Don't make assumptions.

4. Always do your best.

To read the words, they seem like common sense, don't they? They seem like basic principles by which we should strive to live our lives. And yet, they can be the hardest thing to do, even without Borderline in the mix. Let's review them in order as they relate to BPD.

Be impeccable with your word.

How often have we said something in the heat of the moment that we later regret having said? How frequently have we uttered the words, "I didn't mean it!"? I readily admit that this is the hardest one of the agreements for me to work with on a regular and on-going basis. It requires a great deal of practice and discipline to even begin to master.

What's the first and most critical piece of this puzzle? Stopping and thinking before you speak. Living with Borderline is generally referred to as riding a roller coaster. Think about what it's like on a roller coaster: a lot of ups and downs, constant motion, huge adrenaline rushes and possibly some nausea. When you're on a roller coaster, do you stop to analyze the structural soundness of the framing? Do you stop to consider the force and role of physics? Most likely you do not. You're simply along for the ride and thrills!

Training ourselves to stop and think while in the midst of an emotional roller coaster is a difficult task indeed. This guide offers a section on "The Five Steps" which will help you teach yourself to take that pause, examine your core issues, explore your viable options and then, ideally, proceed with the healthy choice.

Don't take anything personally.

What? Are they serious? How can they expect us to not take most of this stuff personally?! The first time I encountered this concept in a real-life setting was when I was being "downsized" after my employer moved their headquarters across the country. The person who would be taking over my responsibilities at the new location was, in my opinion, a complete nitwit. And yet, the company chose him over me! How could I not take something like that personally?

The simple fact of the matter was that I was attaching myself too closely to the corporate decision. I was blurring my boundaries. I was too close to the emotional impact of the situation to place myself in their shoes. Once I was able to step back and see things from an impersonal standpoint, I realized that it was a financial decision. That guy was there and I was here. My position wasn't high enough on the corporate ladder to warrant a relocation package, so I was downsized.

We all deal with life's regular frustrations. When we have Borderline to contend with, those frustrations tend to feel as though they are piling up on our shoulders, and we start to wonder if the universe isn't conspiring to target us personally. Once we have the coping mechanisms in place and have practiced them to the point that they become second nature, it becomes much easier to not take things personally.

Don't make assumptions.

With Borderline thinking, assumptions are the first obstacle we need to overcome. Using my employment situation from the previous agreement as an example, the first "error" I made was assuming that the decision to retain the other guy while letting me go was a personal one. I assumed that they thought he was better than me – both as a person and as an employee. Getting rid of that assumption helped me detach and take the decision impersonally.

Assumptions are way more prevalent than you might think at first. The very reason that this agreement is listed is because it is so predominant in daily living, and it's not limited to only those with Borderline. The book – The Four Agreements – was not written specifically for people battling with Borderline, so it's important to remember that assumptions are things that most people deal with on a regular basis. Keeping that in mind is crucial as you become healthier in your own journey toward recovery because you will undoubtedly encounter individuals who are acting on their own assumptions and may even attempt to project them onto you.

By working to eliminate assumptions from your inherent thought process, you'll be better able to stop the assumptions made by others. Having the conscious awareness of the assumptions around you – both external and internal – will help you better respond to various situations and help you make the healthy choice when you examine your options.

Always do your best.

This one seems like a no-brainer, right? Of course we should always try to do our best. But wait! There is no "try" in that agreement! How can we always do our best? Again, the answer lies within the conscious awareness of our thoughts because our thoughts drive our actions. If we are unaware of what we're thinking (or feeling, for that matter) how can we have predictable behavior? How can we be sure that we're making the healthy choice in a given situation? The answer is simple: we can't.

Always doing our best doesn't mean always being perfect. There is no such thing as being perfect, by the way. We can only be the best ME that we can be. Another added benefit to always doing our best is that, even when we "fail," we have the satisfaction of knowing that we did the best that we could given our knowledge, skills and abilities at that particular point in our journey. And when I say "fail," I put that in quotation marks for a very specific reason. I don't believe that anything is a failure when it comes to recovery; it is a learning experience. No one can make the absolute right decision when faced with the thousands of decisions we must make on a daily basis, therefore it is important that we teach ourselves to learn from each situation so that we can build a "learning library." With each experience where we find out that we might have had better results with a different decision, we learn. Hopefully. And the next time we're faced with a similar situation, we can refer back to that "learning library" and we're better prepared to make a healthier or more productive decision. Thus, we continue to grow, continue to learn and we are then automatically doing our best!

Living with these agreements isn't always easy, especially at the beginning as we begin to incorporate them into our consciousness. Simply reading this segment, or even Don Miguel Ruiz's book The Four Agreements, won't make it happen for you automatically. Intellectual understanding of a concept (or four!) doesn't mean it has incorporated itself into your standard operating procedures. It takes a lot of practice!

In addition to practice, it will take a lot of conscious awareness and energy to become more aware of the choices you have available to you at all times; even during times when it feels like there are no choices to be made. We always choose our reaction and our perception. Unfortunately, over time, we as a society have allowed our norms to become so ingrained into our daily lives that we act first and think later. We have done away with, over time, our ability to stop, think and listen before reacting. These agreements offer us an excellent opportunity to take our lives off of auto-pilot and regain control over a great many things.

Furthermore, I think it highly beneficial to know up-front that it will be virtually impossible for a person with Borderline to simply read this chapter and/or Ruiz's book and change overnight. I think it to be highly unrealistic to expect to be able to change thoughts, actions, feelings, beliefs and patterns of behavior automatically overnight through sheer force of will. As I will mention periodically throughout this book, I think that one of the keys to success in working on any of the coping techniques – including the Four Agreements – is to begin working on them retrospectively.

So what do I mean by "working on them retrospectively"? The saying goes that hindsight is 20/20 and it's more true than not. Once the situation has passed, we are less likely to be hopped up on emotion or a rush of adrenaline. Without the urgency of an immediate situation staring us in the face, we are more likely to be able to make rational, logical decisions based on a wider range of facts. We are more likely to be able to think more clearly and make healthier choices.

Since our Borderline ways of thinking and operating have been finely honed over many years (for the most part) it is totally unrealistic to expect to be able to flip a switch and suddenly start operating in an entirely new way. By allowing yourself to make "mistakes" and continue – in a semi-controlled fashion – living the Borderline way, the way you know, the way you've become accustomed to, and picking up one of those Borderline examples and looking at it in retrospect, you'll be doing yourself the biggest favor possible. You'll allow yourself to learn from your own "mistakes."

I could sit here and tell you that in X situation, you need to do Y behavior but what will you really learn? You'll learn what I say, and you may even learn to follow "the gospel according to Joy" but you won't necessarily learn to think for yourself. Imagine what would happen if I were to offer you "solutions" to a pre-defined set of situations in this book and then you encountered something that I hadn't covered? What would you do? How would you cope?

Many self-help books focus on this sort of "help" and offer cut-and-dry solutions to some of the more common problems or situations that come up. These books teach you to follow their rules but don't help you learn for yourself. By taking control over your own life, its unique intricacies and distinctive patterns, by being able to learn basic principles and apply them to your specific scope of experience, you'll be better equipped to handle life's daily ups-and-downs.

To truly and effectively learn the Four Agreements and to be able to successfully incorporate them into your daily, healthy, happy life, you'll need to learn to work backwards. The homework exercises at the end of this chapter offer some crucial insights into your own personal journey toward recovery. I strongly recommend you take the time to work through them. I even recommend that you repeat them periodically to allow yourself the opportunity to see and chart your progression in your journey of recovery.

Homework

- Free-form write about the concepts you've just read about. How did the words make you feel? Do you accept them, at least in theory? Are you able to envision yourself living them?

    – Spend some time and look around you – at school, work, home, family, past – and find examples where someone you know or have encountered has put one or more of these concepts into practice.

- What do you think your life would be like if you were able to incorporate these concepts into your own auto-pilot? How does this feel? Develop an action plan to reach that goal and implement it.

- Write each of the Agreements on a separate piece of paper and for each one, look back in your life – years ago or the other day – and find one example where you did not follow the basic premise of the Agreement.

  - Examine the overall situation, take an impartial look at your behavior (as out of sync with the Agreement) and theorize about how things would have been different if you'd been able to uphold that particular Agreement.

- For a minimum of two weeks time, keep the Four Agreements at the forefront of your awareness. Devise some way to continuously remind yourself of their wording and the intent of each. (A rubber band around your wrist, a note on your day planner, etc.)

  - At the end of that two week period, review your time with the Agreements. Did you feel calmer? Did your conduct change in anyway? Were you able to see alternatives that you might not previously have noticed?

Separation of Stuff

Separation of stuff is one of the more critical aspects of recovery from BPD. It is this separation of stuff that allows us to differentiate responsibility, and thus reduce feelings of guilt and/or feelings of persecution. It is by separating stuff that we become more stable in our inter-personal relationships, and are better able to maintain healthy, mature, adult relationships.

But what does "separation of stuff" really mean? I'm not talking about separating the laundry as you prepare to do a wash. I'm not talking about separating the boys from the girls. I'm talking about the ability to look at a situation or relationship and separate what belongs to each side or person.

Okay, but what does that mean? Let's take a look at an example:

> Maria and Tom have been dating for a while and Maria gets it set in her head that going to the state fair would be an ideal romantic setting. She can picture the two of them wandering around, holding hands, talking and laughing, trying games, going on rides, sharing cotton candy and getting sticky. It's been a number of weeks since the two of them have gone out to have any fun at all. Usually it's been dinner together or some phone calls to keep the connection between the two of them alive. Maria is eager to rejuvenate their relationship.
>
> So Maria tells Tom, "I think we should go to the state fair this weekend."
>
> Meanwhile, Tom has been looking forward to a quiet weekend, home alone, after a long and draining workweek. Due to a pending merger at work, all employees have been doing close to double shifts for the last four months, barely able to take a half day off on the weekends. This is the first chance he's had to have

82   Putting The Pieces Together

> two solid days free of all work obligations, and not only is he looking forward to his down time, his body is almost requiring it.
>
> So Tom tells Maria, "Honey, I don't think so. This is my first weekend off in months and I was looking forward to vegetating on the couch in front of some college football games."
>
> Maria is stunned and hurt because Tom would rather stare at "the idiot box" rather than have a romantic and fun, relaxing time with her at the fair.

The last sentence in that example shows us that Maria has been unable to separate the stuff of their relationship. She is viewing Tom's words and actions as a direct reflection on her worth and value to him as a human being and as a romantic partner. She is unable to see that Tom's stated desire to relax by "vegetating on the couch" is a reflection of his inner self rather than of her inner self.

When a person is unable to separate stuff in a relationship of any sort, they operate under the belief that "HE" and "SHE" came together and merged entirely and formed a new entity called "WE." Put another way, it's as if two cells merged into one and became a large cell but with two distinct nuclei. If pain is inflicted on one nucleus, the other nucleus must feel it as well. If the nucleus of the left-hand side feels, thinks or believes something, then surely the other nucleus must feel, think or believe the same thing because they have been joined together in this cell or relationship.

Relationships – whether they are parent-child, sibling-sibling, co-workers or romantic partners – are never complete mergers of cells into a conglomerate cell with two nuclei. Rather, a relationship is better thought of as two lakes or ponds joined by a small river, creek or stream that has a moveable dam somewhere between over which both parties have control. There is free-flowing sharing of water between the two lakes through this connecting river but at any time, one or the other may decide to stem the in-flow to their lake or out-flow from their lake by adjusting the controls of the dam. There remains a "HE" and a "SHE" with a smaller portion of connection in the "WE" over which both parties have some influence.

Let's carry this analogy a little bit further. Perhaps the "HE" lake has lily pads and rainbow trout, and the "SHE" lake has minnows and seahorses. With the river connecting the two of them, the "HE" lake may end up with a couple of minnows and a seahorse. "HE" recognizes that "SHE" has influenced his environment and "HE" adjusts accordingly to allow these new additions to thrive in the lake. If "SHE" were to attempt to send half or more of her minnows and seahorses, and try to take half or more of his lily pads and rainbow trout so that both of the lakes were exactly the same to show the world that these lakes belong together, it's not likely that either lake would survive such disruption to its individual ecosystem.

Separation of stuff in human relationships is very important. We must be able to recognize where a particular item belongs: a lily pad does not belong over here so let's put it back where it belongs before we devote resources to transplanting it, only to watch it wither and die eventually because it's in the wrong habitat.

Likewise, in the case of Maria and Tom, his "stuff" is that he'd like to sit on his lily pad and watch the rainbow trout swim by for a while. Maria needs to recognize that his decision to stay at home and watch television is his "stuff" and not a reflection of her. While she might be feeling that he no longer cares about what's important to her, she needs to recognize the boundaries of his decision. She must not make assumptions about his decision. She must not go off on a twisted BPD tangent and figure that since he doesn't want to do what she wants to do, that he doesn't care about her at all whatsoever anymore, and she must be a completely worthless, useless, unlovable slug that will never be happy because she's so undeserving.

Tom's decision is Tom's decision. If Maria is concerned that Tom may not care about her any longer, rather than make the assumption, she must ask for clarification. "Tom, is the reason you'd rather stay home this weekend because you no longer care for me?" In so doing, Maria is sharing her "stuff" with Tom: that she is afraid that he no longer cares for her.

The typical Borderline fashion of handling such situations usually involves assumptions, projections and many harsh words based on those twisted thoughts. Therefore, in order to function in a Borderline-free fashion, one must work diligently at separating the stuff of relationships.

Let's try another example:

> Cindy: Suzie, what's wrong?
>
> Suzie: Nothing.
>
> Cindy: Oh come on, I can tell something's wrong. Why won't you tell me?
>
> Suzie: I said nothing's wrong.
>
> Cindy: I can tell you're lying to me. Real friends don't lie to each other, you know. REAL friends can confide in each other! So come on, spit it out, what's bothering you? Is it that Anne's dumping all her work onto you? Is it your mom again? Is she riding you about your financial troubles? Come on Suzie, you know you can tell me anything!
>
> Suzie: JUST LEAVE ME ALONE!

Exercise:

Please take a few moments to re-read the exchange between Suzie and Cindy and reflect upon how similar situations may have played out in your own personal history.

- Is this a separation of stuff issue?
- If so, who has the problem separating relationship stuff? If not, why not?
- Did you handle similar situations as Cindy did?
- What were the results? Did those results please you?
- Were you able to maintain the friendship with your Suzie?
- What might you have done differently?

While the example with Maria and Tom may be easier to understand as a separation of stuff issue because of the dynamics involved, there are indeed variations on the same theme. With Cindy and Suzie, Cindy was unable to respect her friend's inability or unwillingness to share what was going on for her. Cindy asked a question, was given an answer and then proceeded to make the assumption that Suzie was lying. Cindy operated under the Borderline belief that friends share everything, like the giant cell with two nuclei, so if Suzie was really her friend, Suzie would have shared and it was up to Cindy to show Suzie how good of a friend she really was. After all, Cindy knew all of these stressor items in Suzie's life – her mom, her co-worker.

There are times – usually when I'm trying to explain this concept – that I'd been able to come up with a better title or description beyond "separation of stuff" because it is so darn nebulous. After all, "stuff" could be just about anything. And that, I think, is why no other title was forthcoming. "Stuff" pops up all over the place, in every single relationship.

The checker at the supermarket who gives you a snotty attitude: that's his stuff, not yours. He may be having a bad day. Whatever the reason for his lousy attitude, his attitude is his "stuff." The friend who calls to change or cancel plans at the last minute has his or her own stuff behind that decision. It is not necessarily a direct reflection of your value or worth as a human being. Just remember that their sourness is a reflection of their own frustrations, insecurities and fears rather than a direct reflection of your value or worth.

You're Entitled To Have Feelings – Without Justification

You're entitled to have feelings – whatever they might be. If you feel kinky, guilty, weird, strained, out of sorts, depressed, forlorn, out of place, uncomfortable, etc. – whatever it is you're feeling – you are entitled to feel that. If those feelings make it so that you don't want to be around certain people for a specific period of time (short term or life-long) that's your call to make. You don't owe anyone else an explanation about how you feel or why you feel that way... unless you wish to give that explanation, of your own free will, for your own purposes (to get it off your chest, to speak the words, whatever), you are under NO obligation to provide them peace of mind.

Maybe that sounds harsh but it's true. You cannot be responsible for them to understand the depth and breadth of your emotional state. If they read into your declination of attending a function that you're upset, angry, pissed, depressed, hurt, slighted, etc., whatever, that's THEIR stuff, not yours. If the question comes and you don't know what you're feeling, can't pinpoint it with a name, but have an instinctual feeling of "NO!" then that's all you have to say.

Ideally, you'd do so in a respectful way and let them deal with that "no" however they see fit. By removing or refraining from casting blame or spreading the misery, you've really done the best that you could because you've contained your stuff and are allowing them to process their stuff.

Whether or not they understand your declination of attending is their stuff. The good news – nay, the FANTASTIC news, is that you've proved to yourself that you're able to enforce this particular type of boundary with people that have traditionally been a problem area for you.

Don't worry that they don't understand. They may, in fact, NOT understand and there MAY be more questions about this topic in the future. "Did we do something? Should we do something? What can we do? What's wrong?" You get the idea and I think you've heard it all before – just like I have.

If you don't feel like getting into it, you have the right to say so: "I don't feel like talking about it right now but thank you for asking."

- You have the right to hold your feelings to yourself until you feel strong enough to engage in a discussion that would delve into, or merely touch upon those feelings. Just because someone asks does not mean you are required to answer! (What an amazing concept!)

- And then, when you've sorted through things – even if it's just to the point of a simple sentence – and you feel strong/brave enough to speak on the subject, then you can bring up the subject.

"You know the other day when you asked if there was something wrong and I said I wasn't ready to talk about it? [sets the stage to get them on the same emotional wavelength] I don't feel comfortable around you and dad right now, and I'm not sure why."

And then let it sit. Give mom time to absorb, process and respond. It's tough to do the first time. Hell, the first ten times! It gets easier after that.

Homework

Separation of stuff is one of the most important tasks you can practice during recovery.

- Get a sheet of paper and list between one and three situations where you had a Borderline meltdown or were triggered into depression because of the actions of another.

- What did each of you say? Do?

- How were you feeling? Looking back on the situation, can you remember feeling a similar way in any other situations? Is it possible you reacted disproportionately because you were combining similar experiences based on the memory of feelings?

- For each of those situations, make a column for yourself and the other person. Then attribute "stuff" to each side. This "stuff" can be anything: fear, frustration, anger, decisions, etc.

- What can you do on a regular basis to help remind yourself to separate "stuff" as it occurs?

88 Putting The Pieces Together

The Five Steps

What are the Five Steps and how do they help with recovery from BPD? Simply put, they are a quick and easy-to-use set of guidelines for dealing with every situation life hands you. Every situation? Yes, EVERY situation!

1. Stop/HALT

2. Determine the problem.

3. Determine three possible courses of action.

4. Select the one that's best for now.

5. Do it!

Sound simple? It is. And at the same time, it's remarkably hard to get them put into ordinary practice. Before we examine how to best go about incorporating them into your daily life, let's first take a look at the principles behind each step.

Stop/HALT

One of the most common tendencies when in the throes of Borderline is to act impulsively. The fallout from this impulsivity makes our lives traumatic and dramatic. As easy as it sounds, stopping before acting is one of the core things that needs to be learned to successfully overcome Borderline. It is also the last thing to be put into practice.

The word "halt" has been capitalized because it is actually an acronym:

> **H**ungry
>
> **A**ngry
>
> **L**onely
>
> **T**ired

These four basic feelings – whether psychological, emotional or physical – are key stressors to the genuine self, and will generally trigger an overreaction of some sort. Many people in relationships with someone who suffers from Borderline will often remark that their loved one sometimes acts very childish. Some have even gone to the lengths of attempting to pinpoint the Borderline's emotional age, which is usually around six to eight years old.

This may sound offensive to you right now because who would enjoy being called a child when they're a full-grown adult, even an older teenager? Insulting though it may be, it is quite accurate. The goal of this text is to help you learn, grow and mature into a healthy, happy adult. As Dr. Joseph Santoro says in his book, The Angry Heart, the existential paradox is:

> *"We are not responsible for how we came to be who we are as adults. But as adults we are responsible for who we have become and for everything we do and say."*

While you may not have learned to deal with your core emotions (such as being hungry, angry, lonely or tired, plus a myriad of others) you can now choose to become someone who can handle these sorts of things in a healthy, positive manner. It's a learning process, and once you determine that this is the path you wish to take, it becomes easier to recognize the four basic triggers.

Stopping is the first step because without that pause, the impulsivity will continue to drag you back onto the roller coaster of drama. As I've said, this portion of the learning curve will come toward the end. Simply knowing that you should stop doesn't make it any easier to put into practice. It will become something you work on day by day, incident by incident until you get to the point where you're stopping as a matter of course, without conscious thought or reference to the Five Steps.

Determine the problem.

The most common response I hear (and have said myself) is "But there are dozens or hundreds of problems, not just one!" In reality, that may or may not be true. There are indeed times when we are confronted with multiple problems. There are, however, many more times when we manufacture our problems because it's how we've taught ourselves life actually is. We magnify, distort, twist, project and assume that things are bigger or worse than they really are. This step is critical in your journey of recovery because it will allow you the opportunity to examine reality in a more objective, detached, rational fashion.

Think of it this way: the car won't start. Well, what's the first step? Diagnose the problem! You can't magically make the car start without first knowing what's wrong with it, can you? Sometimes there's a process of trial-and-error involved. Other times a visual examination will do the trick. This is the same principle you will be asked to apply to your daily life and the many situations you encounter. You must clearly identify the problem before you can begin to attempt "fix" it. Without knowing where the problem originates, you will spend exhausting amounts of time and energy blindly grasping at straws in a hopeless attempt at fixing some ill-defined thing.

When it seems there are more problems than just one, the best course of action is to get some index cards out and write a problem on each one. This will allow you to examine the options available to you for each situation, and clarify a healthy path for each. Going back to the car analogy, if your fuel injection is clogged and your windshield is cracked and your rearview mirror has fallen off, each of those issues will be addressed differently and separately. You wouldn't slather Gum-Out on your windshield to be able to see out the back window but you would add some Gum-Out to your fuel tank to clear up the injection problem.

Determine three possible courses of action.

This is the step I personally had the hardest time working with because of my tendency to over-analyze and extrapolate on the potential possibilities. Rather than three possible courses of action, I would be stumped and be able to come up with either one (the original impulsive course of action) or dozens of possibilities because "if I do this, then that could happen so if I choose this other one, then that one could happen but what if I try this one and then this other person decides that and then it causes this other thing to happen..." You get the idea.

For this step, it is crucial that you limit yourself to three choices. For this step, it is crucial that you get yourself to determine three choices. In this step, three is your lucky number.

We've touched on "living on the roller coaster" A good roller coaster doesn't have much travel time while level, but wildly takes you from great heights and plunges you into heart-stopping lows. Borderline has likely conditioned you to the two extremes. There is up or there is down. There is no level. There is no grey. There is happy or there is sad. There is no contentment. Finding that third possibility in this step is going to be your salvation because it will be your grey, your contentment, your health.

A helpful way to remember to seek only three possible courses of action is to keep in mind the goal of recovery work. In Borderline, we tend to think in terms of black and white and in recovery, we seek the grey. Black-White-Grey – bingo! You have three possible courses of action now. By having simple things to remember such as this three-word combination, it will be easier to coax yourself into coming up with the three possible solutions when you're stuck at just the one – which is a fairly common occurrence.

Select the best one for now.

In the previous step, I mentioned the tendency I used to have which had me extrapolating countless possibilities. We do not have crystal balls, nor do we have the ability to predict the future. We simply cannot know with any degree of certainty what will happen as a result of a choice we make. It was this uncertainty that made this step very difficult for me to accept because I wanted to be certain. I equated healthy, happy living with always being right, always doing the right thing, becoming perfect in every way—which is just not possible!

The beauty of the Five Steps is that nothing is written in stone. The Steps are fluid enough to apply to every situation life may hand you. If the choice you make doesn't turn out exactly as you might have wished or hoped, simply pull out the Five Steps once more and work them again to help you get closer to the health you seek.

Recovery is a non-linear process, as some of my smarter friends have told me over the years. I admit to having had a rough time compiling this book for you because it is SO non-linear that I cannot say "Do this, then do this, then do that and you'll be free of Borderline." It's a process of learning, trying, practicing, trying again, forgiving of self, learning and practicing some more. No one expects you to be perfect. Please remember that!

Examples for Real-Life Application of The Five Steps:

Should I stay in this relationship?

Yes, only if my partner is able to show a similar level of commitment to making it work as I am.

No, that other person is probably much better and I'll go be with them now.

Yes, at all costs, no matter how adversely either of us is impacted.

Should I take that other job?

No, even though I don't like this current job or the pay. I know what to expect here so I'll stick it out and hope that things get better.

Yes, because anything has to be better than this place!

Maybe, I'd like to hear more about the job, talk to some people who work there and possibly perform the same job, and I'd have to make sure that the move increases my pay, challenges or furthers my career goals.

That person was rude to me!

Be snotty back to them and get caught up in escalating nastiness.

Slough it off, ignore it if possible and go on with your day, hopefully avoiding simmering resentment.

Recognize that they may be having a rough day, inquire if there was something you could do to help them get back on track and ask that they kindly refrain from taking their frustrations out on you in such a manner.

The psychiatrist wants to put me on medication.

Staunchly refuse.

Accept it on a trial basis, do some research about various medications, check with peers about their results on the same medication, evaluate how the medication would benefit you, log any side effects and be willing to speak honestly to the psychiatrist about your likes and dislikes.

Accept it blindly and keep quiet about anything you dislike about the medication.

My brother wants to come out for a visit and stay at my house.

Accept him into your home without hesitation, reservation or rule of the house set in place.

Accept him into your home with the understanding that he respect the rules of your home and clearly outline them in advance, or at the very least, discuss them with him at appropriate times during his stay.

Refuse to have him in your home on the off-chance that he would greatly disrupt your life and schedule.

I hope these examples, with corresponding samples of possible courses of action, have been helpful as guidelines in the core of the Five Step process.

Homework

Do you see value in the Five Step process? If so, why? If not, what do you disagree with or what would you change?

Are you able to envision yourself, one day, being able to use the Five Step process in some (if not all) situations in your daily life?

Pick a situation in your recent past where you feel you could have handled things better or differently.

- Work all five of the Five Steps.

- Even though the situation isn't present tense, still do the first step and check the past situation for HALT.

- For step three, make sure that one of your possible courses of action is the action that you actually took in that past situation.

- Briefly examine how things would have been different had you chosen a different course of action:

    – For yourself

    – For the overall situation

    – For the other people involved in the situation and/or your life at the time.

- Forgive yourself. Do not beat yourself up for not acting on knowledge you didn't have at the time. The past cannot be changed.

- Add this newly discovered concept – possible course of action – to your Learning Library for reference in the future if/when a similar situation arises.

"Lather, Rinse, Repeat." Do the prior exercise at least twice more.

Formulate a plan to remind yourself to review The Five Steps and your homework for this chapter on a regular basis. Perhaps a weekly or bi-weekly reminder. A note on your calendar. Mark the day you pay the paperboy as the day you also review the Five Steps.

As you move forward in your personal journey toward healthy, happy living, work on incorporating The Five Steps into your coping mechanisms at incrementally earlier stages. Rather than settling for always reviewing the steps in retrospect, try to catch yourself earlier in the process and see if you can begin to apply The Five Steps before taking action.

Make notes or create a special journal to mark your improvement as you incorporate The Five Steps into your daily life to remind yourself of the progress you're making.

96 Putting The Pieces Together

Boundaries & Borders

The term Borderline ostensibly was derived from the mental health professional community because the traits indicated in the diagnostic criteria border several different disorders. Diagnostics are further hampered by the fact that Borderline is traditionally found to be co-morbid with other disorders such as manic-depression, obsessive compulsive disorder, post traumatic stress disorder, etc.

A contingent in the Borderline community finds the term to be more applicable to the process of recovery and healthy, happy living. One of the hardest things for someone with Borderline to work with and accept is boundaries. But what is a boundary?

We don't wander around life with fencing around us to clearly delineate personal space or what we find acceptable. If we came equipped with fences to visibly show our boundaries, we might be happier in the long run but since we weren't born with those fences and gates, it's up to us to put them in place. We must design them, build them, paint them and maintain them.

Suppose you're in an intimate relationship and your partner says, "I want you to get your tongue pierced." Further suppose that you're not comfortable with this as a concept. Perhaps you have an aversion to needles; perhaps you have heard horror stories about infections; perhaps you do not feel comfortable with body modification; perhaps you haven't reached a level of trust within the relationship to mutilate a sensitive part of your body for this person. Whatever the reason, you are not inclined to acquiesce to your partner's request.

An Unhealthy Boundary: "I don't really want the piercing but if it's so damn important to you, and if it keeps me from losing you, then I guess I'll have to do it, even if the mere thought of it makes me sick to my stomach."

A Healthy Boundary: "I do not want to get the piercing as you've described it. Perhaps we could talk about why you want this particular thing."

An Unhealthy Boundary Response: "I ask this one little thing from you and you don't care about me enough to even consider it. What kind of partner are you anyway? This is ridiculous. If you won't get the tongue piercing, then we're through – for good!"

A Healthy Boundary Response: "I understand your concerns about the tongue piercing. Perhaps we could discuss some other ways to solidify our relationship in a way that is mutually acceptable."

Boundaries or borders are what separate "me" from "you" and "him" from "her" in a relationship. They are an expression of what you will and will not accept or tolerate.

As you may have already determined from the previous examples, there are two sides to boundaries: giving and receiving.

Receiving Boundaries

We've all been on the receiving end of boundary requests or demands. The odds are pretty good that we haven't handled those situations very well. Something as simple as, "Please don't use profanity around my two year old child" can trigger severe abandonment and/or rejection issues for someone with Borderline. The thought process, if it were contained in the consciousness, might be something similar to: "You don't want me to use profanity. You don't accept the use of profanity as part of who I am. You are rejecting me as a person. That hurts. Screw you!" The resulting drama may include the loss of a long-time friend.

So how do we get better at receiving boundaries? The short and simple answer is to review the Four Agreements. Boundaries are impersonal things and should not be taken personally. A boundary presented from another person is a reflection of their beliefs, wishes and desires. Because you are a separate and distinct person, with your own beliefs, wishes and desires, their boundary is their stuff, not yours. What you choose to do about the boundary you are presented with is your stuff, and will be discussed in detail in the next section about Giving Boundaries.

The key to accepting boundaries really is keeping them impersonal. And yes, it is possible to keep all boundaries impersonal though it will take some time and practice. Let's look at some examples to help illustrate how to "re-train your brain" to respond to these boundaries.

> **John says:** "You're acting irrationally. Please go home until you can act like an adult."
>
> **Healthy Internal Receipt of Boundary:** "John thinks I'm being irrational. Whether or not I am being irrational, that is his belief and he's entitled to his opinion. He's asked me to go home until some time has passed and we can better communicate. He has not said that he never wants to see me again; he has not called me any names; he has not ended the relationship. He's putting things on hold until the emotion passes. I can live with that because I think it will be better all the way around. While he's under the impression that I'm being irrational, I don't think I could say anything to sway that right now."

Let's review another one.

> **Sister says:** "I don't think it's a good idea for you to stay here when you visit because of the chaos in our house right now. I know of a nice hotel nearby; would you like the number?
>
> **Healthy Internal Receipt of Boundary:** "My sister doesn't want me to stay at her house when I come into town. She says that there's a bit of chaos in her home right now and I can understand her not wanting that increased by my presence. She hasn't said that she never wants to see me again; she hasn't said any hateful things; she has even offered to help me find a place to stay in lieu of her home."

And one more.

> **Spouse's Action:** {makes a face when you make a comment and walks out of the room}
>
> **Healthy Internal Receipt of Boundary:** "Well it would appear that my comment didn't go over very well. I'll interpret his/her leaving the room as an indicator that he/she wants to be alone for a while. When he/she is ready, he/she can talk to me or I can wait a while and approach him/her to see if he/she is ready to discuss whatever it is that's bothering him/her."

100 Putting The Pieces Together

Hopefully these examples have helped shed light on how to effectively re-train your brain, or overwrite those old tapes that probably play in your head. Don't get me wrong – simply reading a couple of paragraphs and reviewing a couple of examples won't make things change overnight. Remember that it took years and years to get those tapes ingrained. The challenge during recovery work is to apply the first of the Five Steps and Stop/HALT to give us pause long enough to be able to detach and remove the feelings of personal attachment from the external statements and actions we receive.

I picked the above examples because they seem to be indicative of the types of boundaries we encounter on a regular basis, though sometimes it's possible that those around us have been conditioned by our erratic behavioral responses to boundaries that they tiptoe around issuing boundaries so we may not be accustomed to seeing them displayed in such concise ways as these examples. I'm sure we can all relate to the gut, visceral, Borderline reactions with which we would ordinarily respond. These Borderline reactions might include screaming, yelling, crying, throwing things, ending relationships, storming out of rooms, destruction of relationship-related mementos, etc.

Remember that there is a difference between a reaction and a response. With Borderline, the response is often the same as the reaction because there is no logical, rational thought process; we operate on auto-pilot. When we become conscious of receiving boundaries in a healthy way, we learn to distinguish between the reaction – the gut instinct – and the response – the external manifestation of behavior and language. There will be times, further down the recovery road, when the reaction will be vastly different from the response.

For instance, just the other day at the office, I encountered a situation which gave me a reaction of shock, anger, disbelief and outrage. The response that I gave, though, was of calm acceptance; I thanked the person and went about my day. In the past, I would have burst into tears and started yelling which probably would have gotten me fired. By accepting that the person was sharing what she considered acceptable, I was able to detach from that and know that it wasn't necessarily a character assassination. It was a boundary and request that I conduct myself in a different fashion. I can now choose to alter my behavior so that I keep my job and never again have to endure that "talk," or I can choose to remain belligerently defiant, continue in my old behavior patterns and accept the consequences of that behavior. It is the ability to detach from the issuance of the external boundary, the skill to Stop/HALT and the application of the principles of the Four Agreements that will best assist you to accept boundaries in a healthy fashion.

Giving Boundaries

An inherent tough spot for people with Borderline is finding self-respect and determining self-worth in light of external circumstances. Borderlines tend to value themselves through the eyes of another – whoever happens to be around at the time – mother, father, sister, brother, lover, spouse, cousin, co-worker, boss, best friend. When we believe the other person wants something from us – whether it's an action, words, or something else entirely – we instantly equate our value to that person with the results we believe we're expected to produce. We are, in essence, afraid to say no. We squash our core beliefs in order to gain acceptance by the other person because we believe that by making the other person "happy" we'll find happiness too.

As we begin to come out of the Borderline "fog," and slowly incorporate healthy coping techniques and responses into our Learning Library, one of the toughest techniques to grasp is that of giving boundaries. Before we can give a healthy boundary, we must first have recognized what a boundary is. Generally, since we've not really had them in our lives, it's best to rely on the issuance of boundaries from others to help us formulate a general idea of what a boundary looks and feels like. As we do the work described in the previous section on accepting boundaries, we should concurrently be making note – either mentally or in a journal – of the various displays of boundaries. By adding these external examples to our Learning Library, we're better prepared to begin giving boundaries to other people.

One of the most common questions for someone at this stage of recovery, as they begin to tentatively explore the possibility of issuing boundaries to those around them is, "How do I know that my boundary request is reasonable?" That truly is the most unsettling part of recovery because we are suddenly very unsure of ourselves. This is the moment in time where we stand on the precipice, unsure of what will happen when we step off the edge. – Will we free-fall and go splat? Will we simply end up taking a single step down, on solid granite, still comfortable and secure but ultimately in a different place?

It's not easy to accept boundaries from an external source in a new fashion, but it's much more difficult to feel strong or brave or secure enough to take a piece of our internal selves and put it out into the world as a boundary. By saying, "This is unacceptable to me," we are sharing with those around us some core beliefs from our genuine self. That sharing is risky because they may reject the boundary; they may reject us as a person; they may laugh at our belief system or our tolerance level. Since we are relatively new to being comfortable with our core belief system, we may feel like a newborn foal, clumsy and unsteady as we try to get our legs. What we "knew" for years or decades to be "the truth" about how to handle a certain situation is now, for all intents and purposes, "wrong" and we're being called on to reformulate a whole new way to express those inner beliefs. There are many doubts and fears at this stage because it truly feels as though we're newborns.

At this time we should begin to rely a little more heavily on our support system and role models.

- "Is this how Annie would handle this situation?"
- "Is this what Joe would say to this person?"
- "What do you think – is this a reasonable thing to ask in this situation?"

I also strongly encourage you, as you seek outside reassurance that you are on-track with healthy boundaries, that you delve a little deeper than accepting a simple yes or no answer. If it's an internal monologue, try to imagine why Joe would say that specific thing in that particular way. Is he covering his bases against further discussion with which he doesn't wish to deal as a result of the boundary? Why would Annie choose to walk away in that situation – to protect herself from physical repercussions, to diffuse the situation, to give herself time and space to regain her equilibrium?

In direct conversations, depending on the support system you have, it may be perfectly acceptable to ask for an example of how to phrase a boundary. Realize, though, that your support person may turn it back to you in the Socratic method of teaching which can, oftentimes, be frustrating. They may very well hand it back to you by saying "Well, what do you think you should say?" And then they may ask further questions designed to help you make the connections yourself: "Now that you've said you don't want them around, do you think there's any benefit to putting a time limit on that banishment up-front?"

Let's take a look at some examples of healthy boundary giving.

> **Boyfriend says:** "I want you to get a tattoo of my name on your butt."
>
> **Healthy Boundary:** "I won't do that because I am opposed to that sort of body modification. Why do you ask for such a thing? Are you concerned about my commitment to our relationship?"

> **Sister says:** "I'm going to be in town on a business trip and I thought I'd stay at your house."
>
> **Healthy Boundary:** "Well, it will be fantastic to see you but right now is not a good time for you to stay with us. The kids are sick and the dog is dying. Won't your company pay for hotel accommodations nearby so we can still get together a couple of times while you're here?"

> **Parent says:** "You really should come to more family functions. I think you really need to be here for Thanksgiving dinner because you're drifting away from the family, no one knows anything about you anymore!"
>
> **Healthy Boundary:** "My relationships with my relatives are my concern and I will manage them as I see fit. Is there something else that's bothering you? Are you afraid that people will think you a poor parent because I don't show up?"

In each of these cases, there is no overreaction in the precipitating comments or requests. No assumptions are made about the "actual intent" of the statements. The causal statements are taken at face value and no mind-reading is employed. Questions are asked to probe because each initiating factor seems to rely on deeper hidden meanings, and knowledge is power. By uncovering the true issue behind the request, you and the other person are better able to work toward resolution rather than allowing the situation to escalate to a point where the relationship is damaged irreparably.

Taking Things At Face Value

We have reviewed the Four Agreements, and at this time I'd like to add something to that list of wisdom. Taking things at face value is, in my opinion, an extension of two of the agreements: make no assumptions and be impeccable with your word. We have learned that it is counterproductive to make assumptions about the actions of others, so let's apply that to their words as well. If someone says something to you, take it at face value and make no assumptions about it. Trust that they, too, are being impeccable with their word.

The reason I bring this up to, so far from our original discussion about the Four Agreements, is that this theory can help you tremendously when you initially begin to work with boundary issues. By accepting the words at face value – regardless of your past interactions with this person, despite your prejudices when you hear certain words – you will be better equipped to deal with the words on a less emotional level.

Back in Chapter Nine, we looked at an exchange between Cindy and Suzie.

> **Cindy:** Suzie, what's wrong?
>
> **Suzie:** Nothing.
>
> **Cindy:** Oh come on, I can tell something's wrong. Why won't you tell me?
>
> **Suzie:** I said nothing's wrong.
>
> **Cindy:** I can tell you're lying to me. Real friends don't lie to each other, you know. REAL friends can confide in each other ANYTHING! So come on, spit it out, what's bothering you? Is it that Anne's dumping all her work onto you? Is it your mom again? Is she riding you about your financial troubles? Come on Suzie, you know you can tell me anything!
>
> **Suzie:** JUST LEAVE ME ALONE!

Let's try that again, but this time, both women will take the others' words at face value.

> **Cindy:** Suzie, what's wrong?
>
> **Suzie:** Nothing.
>
> **Cindy:** Okay. If you want to talk later – about anything – I'll be here.
>
> **Suzie:** Thanks.

Rather than Cindy assuming that Suzie was hiding something from her, the "nothing" was taken at face value. The odds are pretty good that Suzie is comforted by Cindy's response in the second scenario whereas she was pretty upset in the first one.

Let's take a look at another example where taking things at face value can be helpful.

> **Tom:** I think you should go home now.
>
> **Jill:** Why? What did I do?
>
> **Tom:** Nothing, I just don't feel well.
>
> **Jill:** Well you were feeling fine earlier, and you seemed more than fine yesterday when you were over at the neighbor's house flirting with that sleazy woman!
>
> **Tom:** Well, I don't feel good now. I think you should go home because I can't handle this right now.
>
> **Jill:** So I mean nothing to you, is that it? FINE! You miserable son of a bitch, I hope you get pneumonia!

While this is a fictitious example, it seems to be very typical of a Borderline reaction. I know I've had reactions like this personally, and I've spoken to hundreds of people who are in relationships with folks who have Borderline and, well, the above example is all too common I'm afraid.

In that example, Jill was unable to take Tom's word that he was sick. She made assumptions that he was lying, apparently to hide his secret attraction to another woman. Jill exaggerated the assumed situation in her mind – all within moments – and felt the hurt (based on the assumptions) very quickly. She never took the time to process or examine the (perceived) hurt, so she was never able to challenge her twisted thinking and proceeded to the retaliation phase – wishing Tom would end up with pneumonia.

Let's try again, where Jill takes Tom's words at face value:

> **Tom:** I think you should go home now.
>
> **Jill:** Why do you think I should go home?
>
> **Tom:** Because I'm not feeling well.
>
> **Jill:** Is there anything I could do to help you feel better?
>
> **Tom:** No, I don't think so. I think a good night's sleep will help. I'll call you tomorrow.
>
> **Jill:** Okay, sleep well. I hope you feel better. I'll talk to you tomorrow.

Obviously, in the second example, the relationship between Tom and Jill is preserved. Both have taken each other's words at face value and Jill has respected the boundary that Tom set forth: alone time to recuperate from an illness. If Jill still has concerns about Tom's apparent interest in the woman next door, she should work the Five Steps. Her conversation with Tom about his actions in relation to the other woman would be non-accusatory – they would be simple statements of fact and/or first-hand observation. "I saw you over at her house. Why were you there?" And then Jill would allow Tom to answer the question before she asked another. She would receive his response and, yet again, work the Five Steps based on the new information she's received. She can choose to believe him when he says it was a platonic visit to return a borrowed tool, she can accuse him of lying or she can take a wait-and-see approach to see if there are any further suspicious activities between the two of them. If, down the road, Jill has further reason to suspect Tom of infidelity, she will likely take appropriate action – again, based on the Five Steps.

The point here is that when we take people at face value and our inner reactions don't agree with the words we're hearing, the end result is generally OUR stuff, rather than theirs. This is a key indicator that it is probably time to pull out our Learning Library and sift through it to see what has worked in the past when we've felt a similar way. When there is discord between, for lack of a better analogy, our heart (emotions) and our mind (rational logic), it is definitely time to Stop/HALT and work with the recovery tools we've learned before taking impulsive action. Many a relationship can be saved this way. Many a job can be salvaged by learning to recognize the cues. Many a situation can be diffused and worked out to peaceful resolution when at least one person is aware of the dynamics at play.

Perhaps, since you're the one reading this book, you're wondering why it seems as though it now always has to be you who picks up on these things and pays attention to the dynamics. It seems kind of unfair, doesn't it? Well, truthfully, as I've pointed out before:

> *"The unexamined life is not worth living."*
> *~ Aristotle*

Those who've not had to deal with Borderline as part of their daily struggles already picked up on the coping techniques we're discussing and learning about in this book. They did so inherently. It was incorporated into their growing-up experience. In essence, they've been on autopilot and you're being asked to not only fly the jumbo jet, but also explain how it maintains altitude. It's a lot to learn and yes, to a degree, it is unfair; but think of it this way: which of you has more knowledge about who the genuine self is and what makes a healthy, happy life: ? You – who's done all the hard work – or the other guy – who's been coasting on autopilot?

Homework

- Set a timer for twenty minutes and brainstorm about boundaries. Write down or type out anything and everything that comes to mind. Ask yourself questions about the information we've covered in this chapter to help prompt yourself if you get stuck.

- Examine your role models and your support system. Spend some time analyzing instances where any of these people provided you with boundaries.

    – What did that person do?

- What did they say?

- Looking back on the time when the boundary was issued, how did you feel when you received the boundary?

- From a detached perspective and without the immediacy of the moment to interfere, how do you feel about that boundary now?

- What are some things or areas of your life that could use better boundaries? Work, home, friends, school, kids, etc. are all areas in which you could examine for boundaries. Also examine statements you may hear on a regular basis that have "always driven you crazy" when you hear them.

  - Pick between three and five areas or statements and write each of them on a separate piece of paper.

  - For each one, work the Five Steps and include at least two attempts at voicing boundaries in Step Three.

  - Bounce some of attempts at boundary setting with some of the people in your support system and/or your role models. Be open to constructive criticism and honest feedback.

- Refine your boundary attempts and practice saying them. Stand in front of a mirror for a couple of them, and get the feeling of making eye contact while you state your boundaries.

12 Letting Go

There are a few different aspects of the phrase "letting go" which need to be addressed for recovery from Borderline to be effective.

Letting Go of the Comfortable Known

Recovery from Borderline Personality Disorder essentially requires a total reconstruction of thought patterns, inner dialogue and outward responses. A Change in any facet of life produces anxiety. As we begin to accumulate the tools necessary for this reconstruction of the genuine self, we're inevitably faced with a feeling which can be described as "standing on the edge of a cliff, teetering in the dark." That is to say, we're unsure of what will become of us. As is natural, we're petrified of stepping off that cliff. We're filled with terror at the thought of stepping off what we've come to know as solid ground and into the unknown.

When a baby bird gets ready to learn to fly, its mother simply nudges it from the nest and the bird is forced to rely on its own wings and abilities or it will plummet to the ground. We Borderlines don't have that mother bird any longer. We no longer really have anyone shoving us from the nest. We're generally grown adults, or at least in our late teenage years, and we're no longer overly protected or watched over by an adult eager to help us reach the next stage of our development. We're on our own. Without that mother bird standing behind us, pushing and nudging, it then becomes solely up to us to get ourselves out of that nest, off the cliff, from the comfort of the known into the unknown. And that's a mighty tough thing to do!

While there are so many different "shades" or variations of Borderline manifestation, some things remain strong commonalities. The fear of letting go of the comfort of Borderline has to be one of the most common. I've likened this time of transition to suddenly being told that you may no longer use your legs. Your legs are still functional and could get you from Point A to Point B but suddenly you're not allowed to use them. Everything you've ever done – gone to the store, stood in the shower, driven the car, walked the dog – now has to be done in a completely new way. Every method of getting through your normal daily routine is now faced with these challenges. It doesn't make sense, especially since the legs still work and you could easily do all your normal chores, and a whole lot faster.

As you progress through your recovery process, you accumulate tools to help you lead the healthy, happy life toward which you're striving. (These tools will be discussed more in-depth in upcoming chapters.) Consider the hammer and the screwdriver. They are simple in nature but can be used in so many different ways. There are different types and sizes of tools; some require more force than others; some require special knowledge for use. Becoming adept with the tools in your recovery toolbox will take practice andover time; you will not be a master craftsman simply by picking up a single tool. And no one expects that of you!

As you face letting go of the comfortable known, or more simply, the Borderline behaviors that have gotten you this far, there is no expectation of perfection. It took you years to perfect your use of the unhealthy Borderline coping mechanisms, and it will likely take you years (though significantly less) to get the hang of the healthy coping mechanisms, or tools. If you feel perfection is expected, you need to know that this is an unrealistic goal that you're setting for yourself. No one else is setting the bar that high.

As the baby bird first leaves the nest, it does not soar gracefully through the skies. Rather, he sputters and coughs, just barely making it to the ground safely. It will be years before he soars and it will take much practice for him to get there. Likewise, when you face the moment of stepping off that cliff of comfort, you must realize that you will not soar smoothly into the skies of your life. It will also take practice for you to master these techniques, simple though they may be.

The baby bird inherently knows that birds are capable of flying because it has seen others of its kind flying. The same applies to those with Borderline. The techniques work. The tools will get you there. Others have done it, have proven it and, have reached the level of soaring. Trust that it IS possible!

I'd like to share with you now something that I wrote just prior to my diagnosis of Borderline, and subsequent to the journey of self-discovery and healing. I believe it relates to this very topic.

The Cliff – *Part One*

*She stands solitary
alone
but not lonely
at the end of the path
past the trees
at a clearing,
the tips of her toes
perched at the edge
of the cliff
loose rocks surround
her bare feet
the wind is gusting
whipping her long hair
lashing her face
rain washing over her
mixing with her tears
her dress clinging
to her shivering body
she is numb
she is alive with feeling
she is in turmoil
her arms crossed
hugging herself
not from the cold
or the wet
holding the feelings
to herself
she raises her face
to the heavens
closes her eyes
opens her mouth
tastes the rain
swallows the nourishment
of the earth
gaining strength from it
feeling the wetness
on her face
trickling down her neck
running between her breasts
raising her hands
to her face
she wipes the water away
futilely
she is weak
she is troubled
she is dangerous
looking over the cliff
down the face
the sea crashes against
jagged rocks
sending spray toward her
she leans forward
a bit
her feet unsteady
her legs weak
the wind strong*

The Cliff – *Part Two*

closing her eyes
swaying
teetering
on the brink
a crow sounds in
the trees behind her
snapping her out of
the reverie
steadying herself
she turns slowly
checks behind her
clouds making the path
dark
obscured
hazy
she does not need to see
she knows from where
she has come
to her left is a path
gravel
unsteady
winding
to her right is a path
paved
smooth
straight
the end of either
is not in sight
they are continuous
each
she turns back to the cliff
desperation
despair
despondency
she sinks to her knees
hands cover her face
weeping
sobbing
shaking
she knows she cannot
stay here
to do so would be
certain death
she must move
this she knows
the indecision is
overwhelming
frightening
terrifying
she cannot go back
she cannot go forward
she
must
choose

The Cliff – *Part Three*

just within her reach
just before her
an oddly shaped stone
feeling it between her fingers
rolling it in her hands
touching it to her lips
clutching it to her chest
grasping it firmly in one hand
it fits perfectly
molded to the contours
within its confines
it is alive
it gives her more strength
to the side of her
a gnarled branch
worn smooth from time
and elements
slowly running her fingers
across its length
feeling the ageless beauty
firmly grasping it in her hand
she uses it for support
as she raises herself
from the earth
stone in hand
branch for support
she has made her
decision
she takes a few
tentative steps
down her chosen path
hesitating
faltering
feeling the strength
of the elements
around her
within her
of her
she heads
purposefully
confidently
fearlessly
down
the
chosen
path.

Letting Go of Pain & Relationships

This aspect is a little more complicated but just as critical to recovery from BPD. As we will explore in further detail in Chapter 13, it is very difficult for someone with Borderline to let go of certain things, usually negative things. This clinging attitude must be abandoned in order to move forward into healthy, happy living.

Parents

Oftentimes, one of the largest issues for people with Borderline is their relationship with parents. Rather than blaming our parents for the manifestation of BPD in our lives, we need to do a couple of things that will assist us in getting closer toward recovery.

First, we need to recognize what we actually had as children. We should recognize the abuse – physical, verbal, emotional and in some cases, sexual – and we should also work toward counteracting that with any positives we can find in our pasts. It is important that we face what our past consists of because, when we choose to deny what happened to us, we are unable to conquer our fears of those old memories.

Next, we need to step back and look at who we are now. Are we still six years old? Will we get severely punished if we say a curse word? No. We are (for the most part) adults, living our own lives, holding down jobs, maybe even with families of our own. We no longer have domineering and/or unstable parents ruling our lives. We are the only ones in control of our day-to-day living.

As we assess these two things – turbulent childhood and control over adulthood – we may be faced with an inner-conflict. When we recall these aspects of our childhood, we feel the feelings we felt then. They may be overwhelming. The most common refrain I hear when dealing with this particular issue is "She never loved me like I wanted/needed!" or "He never treated me like a loved child." This may very well be true.

One of the more difficult things we are asked to do in recovery is to accept that we didn't get the love we wanted or needed as children. (We'll discuss more about acceptance in the next chapter.) Accepting that we didn't get the love we wanted or needed is the first step of letting go of that childhood pain. We recognize that the Child Us was deprived or abused and we recognize that the Adult Us is no longer the Child Us. We recognize that we cannot change the past, and we recognize that we can move forward forging a better, happier, healthier life for ourselves as we now have the control.

Letting go of the past, our childhood, our hurts doesn't mean forgetting the past. It simply means that we no longer live – long-term or temporarily – as the Child Us, with the child's emotional reaction. We claim our personal power.

Friends & Intimate Relationships

As adults with Borderline, we continually face abandonment issues. Even when we reach the point where a mental health professional decrees that we no longer exhibit Borderline traits, we will still face the ending of relationships. Friends move away. Relatives get divorced. Jobs end. We are continually subjected to the loss of relationships in our lives. This is a reality of life to which we must surrender. It is a reflection of our relative mental health when we are able to accept the loss with grace and dignity rather than outrageous responses such as revenge, stalking or even a suicide attempt – all of which are traditional Borderline reactions to loss.

It helps a great deal if we can grasp the concept of fluid relationships on an intellectual level at a non-emotional time in our lives. For instance, look back at the third grade. With whom were you friends? Who did you know at that time in your life? Are they still an active part of your life? The odds are pretty good that they've dropped out of your life at some point in the past years or decades. Likewise, people who are in your life right now may not be active members of our social lives in the future.

Simply knowing that loss is inevitable isn't enough. We also have to be able to remind ourselves that this loss is part of the process of living. This isn't to say that we should live with a continual sense of doom and gloom that relationships don't generally last for decades, but that we should be aware that there is a natural cycle to all things in life. We are born, we live, we die. We work, we pay taxes, we get a refund. (If we're lucky!) Winter, spring, summer, fall. Daylight, dusk, night, dawn. It's all a cycle. Yes, it's sad when we can no longer wear shorts and bikinis but we exchange that for hayrides and apple cider. And then we exchange that for a roaring fire and snow angels. And that gives way to April showers and May flowers. When one thing departs, it leaves room for something new to arrive, to be explored, to be shared, to be enjoyed. By spending an entire season pining away for the carefree days of summer, we miss the glory of fall. By pining for a lost love, we miss new opportunities for love.

There is naturally a grieving process when any relationship ends. We mourn the loss of the person's presence in our lives. We grieve the loss of potential future good times. We savor the actual good times that are now tinged with bitter sweetness. We accept that the relationship is over; and it is this step that is so crucial to mental health, as will be more closely examined in the next chapter. And we begin to move on, also a crucial aspect of recovery and healing.

Letting Go of Outcomes

Expectations. They seem to be a natural part of the human condition and yet they can be very harmful, if we let them. We expect that our paycheck will be there, correct, on Fridays. We expect that our neighbors will be friendly, or at least civil. We expect that our children will behave themselves, obey the law and respect their elders. We expect that the sun will rise and the seasons will change. We continually surround ourselves with expectations so it's little wonder that, with Borderline, we get thrown for such a loop when our expectations are dashed.

When dealing with other people, as we must as human beings, we need to relearn how to work with our own expectations. The first, and arguably the most important, thing we must keep in mind is that we have expectations ... and so do other people! You have the right to your expectations; they have a right to their expectations. Most often, those expectations are not exactly the same. Many times, those expectations are widely divergent and you may find that you and the other person are working at cross-purposes.

Trust is a difficult thing to learn: trust in self; trust in the universe; trust in outcomes as a natural extension of the preparatory steps. I use episodes of the old television show "MacGuyver" as a guiding force in my life. In one of the episodes, someone asks the title character about his plan. He gives a very loose & vague plan. The other person is astonished that he hasn't put more detail into the plan. The character's response is along the lines of, "The more you limit yourself on the details, the more likely it is things can go wrong. The fewer the details the more room for flexibility and a positive outcome."

We cannot become what we need to be by remaining what we are.

We need to be able to allow change into our lives in order for change to happen. By stubbornly clinging to the present – whether because it's comfortable or out of fear of the unknown – we remain stagnated in the same, continued misery we profess to want changed. That change has to begin from within in order to be effective. Simply wanting things to change around us will not automatically make things within us change – however – changing things within us will cause those external things to change automatically!

Using an excerpt from The author of the book *Dark Moon Mysteries*, a book with a decidedly metaphysical tone, when discussing the purpose of meditation, the author had this to say:

> "If, for example, you light a green candle every day to create some sort of change, this would be working from the outside to the inside. You light the candle in order to create a change in consciousness. You do not have to concentrate on creating consciousness changes because the physical candle becomes a psychic trigger, setting the internal powers of the unconscious in motion."
>
> "If you begin meditation work from the point of the unconscious – for example, by meditating on the purpose of lighting the green candle – you are working from the inside to the outside. By meditating on the purpose, you do not necessarily need the green candle because you begin with a shift in consciousness. However, meditation that does not translate into action is useless."

I share this excerpt to highlight the fact that in order to truly achieve a healthy, happy life, we must learn to work from the inside rather than from the outside. Look for the answers within yourself rather than seeking answers or validation from the outside. The various coping mechanisms introduced and discussed in this book will, ideally, become your personal set of green candles.

At the beginning, you'll need to work with the actual green candles, or keep the reminders of how to work the coping techniques at the forefront of your daily life. With time and practice, you'll be able to shift your consciousness automatically – by accessing that Learning Library – and merely reflecting, however briefly, on your wide array of green candles or healthy coping techniques without as much preparation, formal settings or assistance from outside sources. It will originate and emanate from within. Furthermore, when we begin to trust in ourselves, in the solidity of our belief system, trust in our actions, the outcomes will generally be aligned with our overall goals of healthy, happy living.

Forgiveness

Why would I bring up the topic of forgiveness in the section about letting go? The answer lies within being able to let go of the pain and resentment we've harbored for a long time. A wise person once told me:

> *Harboring resentment is like swallowing poison and waiting for the other guy to die.*

Holding onto pain, grudges, anger and resentment are not healthy and, as such, have no place in our new, recovered, healthy, happy lives. In order to get to that place though, we must put a lot of the techniques we have learned thus far into practice. Then we have to really work hard to give up the comfortable known of being angry at that particular person.

Think about it – we may have spent ten or twenty years angry as all get-out at our mother who beat us, the uncle who molested us, the stranger who raped us, the justice system that did nothing to protect us … you get the idea. It is very difficult to suddenly be confronted with this alien notion that we should forgive these people for their heinous transgressions against us.

Here's something else to think about: personal power. The odds are pretty good that the individual who wronged you so grievously is not in your presence twenty-four hours per day. They may have passed away; they may live in another part of the country; you may only run into that person at family gatherings a few times a year; you may never have known the person's identity, and have never encountered him (or her) since. And yet, you continue to devote so much of your time and energy to thinking about the person, their actions, vengeance, retribution or justice. They may not be physically present but yet, to you, it's as if they follow you everywhere, all the time. Wouldn't it be nice to be free of that haunting?

We have talked about The Four Agreements. Don't take that person's actions personally. We have talked about Separation of Stuff. Their actions toward you were their stuff; your continued resentment of them is your stuff. You cannot change the past and you cannot change who that person is today. The only thing over which you have any control is yourself, how you will choose to live from this day forward, how much of your personal power will you will continue to hand over to this ghost from the past.

Letting Go   119

Forgiveness doesn't mean forgetting. Letting go of the past hurts doesn't mean pretending they never existed. The goal here is for you to separate your present-day self from the wounded-child-self-of-the-past. That child or teenager endured those unimaginable wrongs; that cannot be changed. But you are no longer that wounded child; you are an adult. It is within your power now to become the strong, healthy, confident and happy adult that you have the potential to become, and in so doing, you will make that wounded child gleefully happy. You survived and you soar in the skies. You are not still cowering in the corner, scared of every shadow, afraid to live, petrified of that person who wronged you.

The vast majority of crimes and abuse situations are primarily based on control. The attacker is after total control and complete domination over the victim. In this case, you were the victim and your vindication, the "punishment" to that attacker, is that they no longer have that control over you. By forgiving them their actions, by letting go of the hurt, by leaving behind the wounded child but not forgetting, you have dominated the situation that has haunted you, likely for years.

Yes, what happened to you was wrong. Yes, that person should be punished and brought to justice. Heck, even a sincere, heartfelt apology would be nice. Without relying on the expectation that any of those external sources of potential comfort will happen, you must work toward accepting what happened to you in the past, hold tight to the Four Agreements, work the Five Steps and separate the stuff that's been swirling around within you for years.

Without knowing your particular situation, but based on countless conversations with literally hundreds of people, I would hypothesize that the actions that happened to you were based on the other person's stuff. That is to say, they themselves were mentally unhealthy; they were after complete control and total domination; they were transferring anger toward someone else onto you because you were close, handy, walked in at the wrong time, whatever. I think it extremely unlikely that there was anything you did to warrant such treatment.

If you disagree with my statement about your role as a precursor to the injustices brought to you, I strongly encourage you to speak with a qualified and competent therapist.

Forgiveness toward those who wronged you is about accepting that their actions were their stuff, not yours. Without forgiveness toward those who wronged you, your life will always be tied – by chains and concrete – to the moment of the injustice. Allow me to say it again: forgiving them does not mean forgetting what they did. It means understanding that they alone were in control of their actions; their actions were wrong. The past cannot be changed and you are no longer living in that moment – you have grown, matured, healed and moved on.

> *"The best revenge is living well."*

Continuing to live in the moment of the abuse is not living well. It is stunted growth and it is unhealthy. The past will always be there, for it cannot be changed. You may always revisit it at any time – an anniversary, a life milestone, a special announcement, reflection and sharing with others to help them in the process, etc. – but you no longer need to live there. By engaging in forgiveness for those who did you wrong, you engage in healing and growth for yourself and those presently in your life.

Homework

You've read the poem titled "The Cliff." Spend some time and reread the piece. Then meditate on the words you've read.

- How do they make you feel?
- Can you envision yourself standing at the edge of that cliff?
- Do you see the connection between the storyline of the poem and the choice you must make between continuing in Borderline behavior and seeking a healthy, happy life?

Have you ever done or tried anything new? Maybe you taught yourself to ski, or ride a motorcycle or moved to a new state without having a job lined up. Reflect on those times you've tried new things.

- How well did those things work out? Were you a master at the activity the first time you attempted it? Did you try again?
- Did you give up on the activity? (Do you still have the skis in the garage, collecting dust?) If so, what were you feeling as you quit? What might you have done differently in preparation for your first attempt at the activity?

Are you able to recognize any abandonment issues in your life? Who do you think abandoned you?

Letting Go   121

- Think intellectually for a while. What do you think their "stuff" was in relation to their decision to separate themselves from you? I encourage you to work on forgiving those people for their decisions. They have and had the right to their own boundaries, just as you yourself do now.

What comes to mind when you think about forgiveness?

- Does it sound scary? Peaceful? Why?

Picture your life as if none of those bad things happened. How does it feel? Are you happy? Carefree?

Do you believe it possible to achieve that feeling of happiness and contentment despite the things that were inflicted upon you? Why or why not?

Putting The Pieces Together

13 Acceptance

If you've made this far into the book, it would stand to reason that you've accepted the diagnosis of Borderline Personality Disorder. Why do you think you did that? Why did you accept it? Did you read enough to recognize, beyond a reasonable doubt, that BPD was the foundation for some, most or all of the issues in your life causing discomfort, disruption or pain?

In my own personal journey, I found that acceptance was one of the crucial things I could do to help myself. Please keep in mind that acceptance does not mean approval. I cannot begin to tell you how important that distinction is. The Serenity Prayer, originally written by Bill W. in 1942, most commonly used in the Alcoholics Anonymous circles, goes like this:

> God grant us the serenity to accept the things we cannot change, courage to change the things we can, and wisdom to know the difference.

I won't go off on a tangent about religion because I believe we all have our own religious beliefs and this book is not about religion; it is about healthy, happy living. This chapter, in particular, is about acceptance so let's focus on the remaining portion of the Serenity Prayer.

Acceptance is very important in the entire recovery process – especially in boundary setting and, of course, boundary acceptance. As you've learned about the separation of stuff, hopefully you've come to understand that other people have stuff – beliefs, hopes, wishes, behaviors, desires, expectations, etc. – that has nothing to do with you. That is to say, that you have no control over their stuff. It is their stuff. They can put it out there in front of you if they choose, or they can keep it hidden from you and operate on a less-than-fully-honest level. That is nothing you can control. When you can get to the point where you accept that people are separate and distinct from you, though their words and deeds may impact you, you'll stop trying to change them for they and their actions are things which you cannot change. The only thing you can change, the only thing over which you have control, is your own responses, words and actions.

Early on in this book, we talked about putting people up on pedestals, where we looked at them and saw them as we wanted to see them rather than as how they really were. This pedestal placement happens all too often in relationships – and not just in relationships where Borderline is a factor. I'd venture to say that many of the divorces in the world are a direct result of pedestals. One person meets another, and either one of them or both of them look to that other person to fulfill whatever fantasy they secretly harbor of what a perfect mate should be. And when I say "secret," it may even be secret from the fantasy-holder's conscious awareness, buried down in the subconscious.

By taking off those rose-colored glasses early in the formative stages of the relationship, both parties are better able to objectively look at their potential mate to see them for what they truly are. There are plenty of stand-up comics who make lots of jokes about how women are the ones who expect men to change. These jokes get the laughs because they are based on truth. Maybe they're not true unilaterally or in every instance, but they're true enough to garner laughter and applause. The desire to change other people is probably ancient and it takes concerted effort to overcome. And the good news is that it can be overcome!

As I said earlier, acceptance does not mean approval. A criminal court can accept that a defendant has committed a heinous crime but that court does not approve of the action. Similarly, a woman can accept that her husband is physically abusive. It then falls to her to decide if she approves of his actions. If she does not, she can and probably should work the Five Steps. Ultimately, a healthy woman would choose to remove her husband from her life – whether by kicking him out of the house or by leaving the home and seeking shelter at various places of refuge.

Expectations are another issue which should be addressed when talking about healthy, happy living. What would you say if I told you that you should never hold an expectation at all, ever? Based on the dozen-or-so times I've put this concept on the table in the past, I could probably predict some of the protestations that I would hear. The truth of the matter is that expectations are relationship killers.

Acceptance   125

While everyone has the right to their own expectations, when overemphasized, they can be relationship killers.

Rather than putting expectations on the table, I encourage you to try a new approach: consequences to actions. Let's do a few examples to highlight the difference between expectations and consequences to actions.

> **Expectation:** Bill, you need to pick up milk on your way home.
>
> **Consequences to Actions:** Bill, could you pick up milk on your way home please? Without milk, I can't make the soufflé I promised you.

> **Expectation:** Jill, stop being so melodramatic for crying out loud.
>
> **Consequences to Actions:** Jill, I can't tolerate this constant melodrama. If you can't communicate in a rational, adult manner, I'll have to end this relationship for my own sake.

When I first began my journey toward recovery, I found myself at an online bulletin board designed to be a sanctuary for people who were trying to cope with a person in their life who was suffering from Borderline Personality Disorder. BPD. Because I was ill-equipped at the time to deal with some of the things I was hearing, I acted out in typical Borderline fashion. I was ultimately asked to leave by the board's owner. I redoubled my efforts to try to change their minds about people with Borderline. I don't know if I succeeded or not but I do know that I learned a lot about consequences to actions at that time. The consequence to my acting out was dismissal from the community. I had options available to me:

- Continue to act out and be a thorn in the board's side.
- Leave with my tail tucked between my legs, rejected and ashamed of my behavior.
- Continue to interact with these people, helping them to understand the process of the Borderline mind, while behaving myself according to the rules of the community.

I chose the last option and I'm glad that I did because, while I was trying to "teach" them how the Borderline mind worked, I concurrently taught myself. That wasn't the first time I'd had consequences imposed on my actions; it was just the first time it made sense to me in the context of BPD. It also wasn't the last time I was faced with consequences to my actions.

When I do volunteer work at the various internet communities in which I am active, I make it a point to work with the theory of consequences to actions. It seems that a basic principle of Borderline is to blame everyone else, the world, life in general, a deity or the dog for bad luck. A common refrain is "Why do these things always happen to me?" Or "How come no one ever sticks around?" As a board administrator (on a team of administrators) I am often called all sorts of names and blamed for sanctions, such as the individual having been banned from the community.

Don't get me wrong: there are plenty of online communities which operate under dictatorships and these individuals take great joy in banning people for speaking up, saying what's on their mind, expressing a dissenting point of view or any of the hundreds of other infractions of nebulous or never-defined rules. Those communities and administrators should be watched out for and steered clear of. However, what we're talking about here is the methodology of administering "consequences to actions."

In the process of recovery, it is immensely helpful to be exposed to such a community or individual. Ideally, this should be someone quite close to you in terms of intimacy, who will not let you "get away with" the typical Borderline antics. I guarantee you that it will be extremely uncomfortable the first time that you are exposed to this method.

I'd like to share with you an anecdote from the discussion board. It is fictitious insofar as it is a compilation of similar events that have happened over the last several years.

> Kelley shows up at the board and begins acting out. Community members reach out to her and try to assist her in seeing a new, different, healthier perspective. Thoughts and ideas are given to her. Kelley outright dismisses and ignores them. Kelley goes further and accuses all those who've interacted with her of being against her for religious reasons. While community members have expressed differing religious beliefs, the comments to her have always been respectful in nature and have politely asked that she show a similar respect for their different opinions.
>
> Kelley's behavior within the community is discussed amongst the administrative team. She is being disruptive but at the same

time, it is helpful to the previously existing members to have her there because they are able to practice separating stuff, posting with impeccable words, not making assumptions about Kelley's words and so forth. However, the decision is ultimately made, after continued BPD antics and several warnings from both community leaders and fellow brethren, that Kelley should lose her access to the community for a temporary period of time.

At the time Kelley's access is revoked, she is told that the community ban is temporary and that she is responsible for how long it will last. It is made clear that the ban is an enforced "breather" and she is encouraged to take some time to reflect on how her actions played a role in the revocation of her access to the community. When she felt comfortable that she had looked within, examined her own behavior and was willing to accept personal responsibility for her actions, she would be welcomed back into the community.

Kelley created a new user name and accessed the community again but this time did not act out. She reviewed the sequence of events that culminated her temporary dismissal. She spent some time reflecting on what she might have done differently. She got to the point where it was no longer "me against them" but rather started to see where she may have phrased a belief differently and gotten a different response. She started to realize that she had been wrong for blaming everyone else and their religious beliefs when she had been, at the time, categorically unable to acknowledge her own responsibility.

Some months after her assisted departure from the community, she contacted one of the administrative team and shared her new understandings and requested re-admittance. Kelley was welcomed back with open arms by the administrative team, team and, understandably, some trepidation from the general population who had been a little shaky themselves during her last appearance. Everyone gave Kelley the benefit of the doubt and soon enough, she proved – through her actions – that she had learned a great deal about personal responsibility.

During her tenure with the community, Kelley had the opportunity to observe other newcomers act out in ways similar to her own initial introduction. Kelley always shared her story – the lows and the highs – and sometimes, not always, but sometimes, she was able to help someone else understand the importance of consequences to actions.

While Kelley was a composite character based on my experiences, every word of the above story was true – as plucked from the original true stories. I'd also like to highlight for you the "enforced breather" and how it mirrors the first of the Five Steps. In the case of Kelley, she was unable to bring herself to Stop/HALT, and continued acting impulsively. The responsible administrator or team of administrators will do what is best for both the individual and the community. Interaction, even heated interaction, is certainly allowed, encouraged and sometimes given wide latitude.

When it becomes counter-productive to either the individual or the community, consequences to actions need to be stated. It is then that the individual has a choice to make. If they have reached the level of recovery where they are able to see that they have more than one choice – say perhaps, three possible courses of action – and needn't continue to act out, then the consequences needn't be imposed. If they have not reached that stage, then, yes, it is my belief that the consequences need to be realized – brought into reality.

Not everyone will operate this way, though. That will make things tough for you because, as much as you'd like to have a black-and-white book of "if this, then that" we live in a world of grey. What bothers one person may not even faze another person. What mildly irritates the neighbor to your left might have the neighbor to the right calling the authorities. This is when the Five Steps play an important factor in your ability to function in the "grey world." If, when you determine your three possible courses of action, you've selected an option that's black, one that's white and one that's grey, the odds are that negative consequences will be greatly minimized if you act on the grey option.

Homework

- Pick a person in your life who does something (or many things) that you would like them to change.

    – Knowing what you do now about acceptance, determine if that aspect of who they are is something you are willing to accept in your life.

    – Work the Five Steps about the issue that concerns you.

- What expectations have you held in any of the important relationships in your life?

    – Were those expectations always met?

- When the expectations were not met, what was the result? How did that impact the relationship?

• How do you deal with situations when consequences to your actions are imposed?

- Does it feel better, more empowering when the actions are defined and the consequences are made clear prior to the sanctions being imposed? Or does it feel just as bad when "punishment" happens "out of the blue"?

• Look back in your life and add things to your Learning Library. List out the truisms you already know. Things such as: If I scream in the middle of the office, there will be some sort of consequence. If I hit my wife, I could go to jail. If I shake my baby, he could die.

- Do you think that all consequences need to be clearly stated for all actions up-front?

- How do you reconcile the "assumption" that an action could have a negative consequence with the Four Agreements?

130 Putting The Pieces Together

14 Self-Talk

"I really shouldn't even bother trying to do this because no matter what I do, I'm always a failure!" This is a prime and classic example of Borderline self-talk. Self-talk is usually negative in nature and is often "heard" in our heads as someone from our past who continually (or at least during important times) engaged in this sort of negativity. It is this self-talk that can be our biggest hurdle to overcome. The negative self-talk has likely been around for years or decades so please don't expect to simply be able to flip a switch and turn it off as you might with a radio or television set.

> *The greatest journey and worst enemy are both within.*

The annoying part of the negative self-talk is that it plays hide-and-seek with us. There are often times when we feel as though we're on top of the world, everybody loves us, and nothing can go wrong. And, true to Borderline fashion, one tiny glitch pops up and we're sent into a terrifying downward spiral. The negative self-talk takes over and we plummet into this dank, dismal abyss of self-loathing, rejection and failure.

As I said, you can't just turn off the self-talk but you can work on counteracting it over time until you reach the point where it's not the driving force of your tough times.

> **Default Negative Tape:** You're alone because nobody really finds you acceptable or fun to be around on a regular basis. You're either too much trouble (too needy/dependent) or too independent (too uncaring of meeting their desires/selfish.)
>
> **Response:** That's not true. I'm alone because this friend is away, and this other friend is working and this other friend already had plans. Their schedules are NOT reflections of my worth or value as a human being.

> **Default Negative Tape:** Oh my God! I'm going to have to do this whole life alone! This is too much for me to handle!
>
> **Response:** Wait. HALT! Let's see if I can come up with ways I can find to surround myself with people so I feel less lonely. Thinking that "how things are right now" is "how things will always be" is twisted thinking. I will take some time to untwist that thinking.

> **Default Negative Tape:** I am afraid of "having to" or "trying to" keep myself entertained during times when I am painfully choosing to be alone (based on abusive relationships.)
>
> **Response:** What is to be afraid of? I'm making the choice to be alone. When this anxiety starts up, I will work on meditation/allowing myself to feel the feelings/talk myself through the fears, etc.

Teaching yourself to overwrite these old tapes will be a challenge – I won't lie to you. They have been insidious in the development of Borderline. In order to fully recover from BPD, you will need to overwrite them. There are no two ways about it. The Being able to recognize when these tapes are playing is the key to recovery to doing this is to be able to recognize when they are playing. So how do you do that? After all, these negative messages are pre-programmed into your autopilot.

The bottom line is that you'll need to become very vigilant in the self-talk you provide yourself. Truthfully, I believe that the only way to change that message over the long-haul is to counteract the negative messages that are already default messages (due to shoddy programming early on) with interactive self-dialogues. Simply getting upset with yourself for having the default negative messages isn't going to accomplish anything, except increase stress and anxiety. It's only, in my opinion, by having the internal monologue on a regular and prolonged basis that will allow your subconscious to begin to believe the positive stuff.

As you become accustomed to catching yourself listening to negative default tapes, you may begin to notice that the messages present themselves in different ways. For instance, "You're a bad person and don't deserve happiness" is different from "I'm a bad person and I don't deserve happiness." When you hear the words and they're in a context which would suggest an external source – perhaps a parent, a sibling, a childhood bully – those messages are the easiest to counteract. They were likely external in origin to begin with and as such, since they've been bombarding you "externally" for years, they haven't necessarily become part of your subconscious. Yes, they're still in there and you may have, over the years, agreed with them, but they've not been originating from within your own subconscious. When you catch yourself hearing, "You're a bad person," try counteracting that with "I AM A GOOD PERSON! I deserve happiness."

Unfortunately, it's been my experience that sometimes people try to counteract their negative self-talk with external positive talk. What I mean by that is that they try to use "You're a good person" as a means of positive self-talk. While I can understand the nurturing aspects of feeling as though there is an external source to the positivism – in lieu of a nurturing parent or loving spouse – it fails in two respects.

First, it doesn't penetrate the subconscious because the subconscious only understands positive "I statements." Hearing positive words from a secondary source does little to nothing for the subconscious. Second, this sort of statement, no matter how positive it might be, is no replacement for actual external validation. If you're truly craving external validation and are expecting the secondary self-talk to fill that void, you will certainly be left disappointed. Please keep in mind that I do not support validation from an external source in lieu of internal validation.

There are layers to this issue and, ideally, the goal would be to self-validate, examine your options, make no assumptions, take people at their word – even and especially if they aren't sharing their words with you – and you'd make a healthy decision about the fate of that particular relationship. However, I know we don't live in a perfect world and nobody is perfect, least of all as they attempt to master self-validation through positive self-talk. It seems to be fairly common to expect that people we care about will validate us.

As such, we usually look to those around us for validation, much as we did when we were small children. "Look what I can do!" The danger in doing this, as adults, is that adults generally expect that other adults can self-validate so they don't bother. When things become dramatic or hit crisis-mode, these adults may be inclined to offer reassurance but again, constant drama or never-ending crises can become tiresome on a regular basis. When that point is reached, we might start to feel as though our support network is crumbling away, and be even more vulnerable to the negative self-talk.

When we are relying on the external sources of validation or positive reassurance that we are good, worthwhile or doing the right thing and it never shows up, it is understandable that we might try to recreate that on our own with those secondary positive self-talk statements, such as "You're doing the right thing." This logic breaks down as we have not eradicated the expectation that validation should be external. We're expecting someone else to tell us "You're lovable" and after a while of telling that to ourselves and not hearing it from a truly external source, we begin to become disgruntled, even resentful and angry, which only serves to exacerbate and compound the original problem. Suddenly we realize that we've merely prolonged external and external-substitutes rather than working diligently toward the truly effective and long-lasting solution of positive first-person self-talk.

Homework

- Spend two weeks with self-talk as your primary focus. Stay vigilant to the inner voices. You don't necessarily need to combat every negative message you hear as you begin this self-talk process. Simply make note of what the original message was and how you responded.

- Pick another two weeks – not necessarily the next consecutive two weeks, it may benefit you to take some time off of this topic to allow your subconscious to assimilate and understand the previous exercise.

    – This time, focus on positively and effectively counteracting the negative self-talk of which you become aware.

    – Make note of the negativity and the positive responses you give.

- Pick another two weeks – again, not necessarily the next consecutive two weeks. Spend some time with your notes from the other two exercises.

    – From an objective and non-immediate perspective, draft the "ultimate" responses to those negative self-talk statements that crop up.

    Review them for positivism.

    Make sure they're in the most effective presentation to be absorbed by your subconscious.

– Add them to your Learning Library.

– Practice saying them – only the positive self-talk statements/rebuttals – aloud. Perhaps say them in front of a mirror while making eye contact with yourself.

- Question those around you. Compare your internal self-talk to their external perception of you and/or your situation. Check with more than one other person. The law of odds then comes into play. If three people think you're worthwhile/lovable/doing well, and you're the only one who does not, who do you think is more on-target?

15 In The Moment

We're all pretty familiar with the feelings of the lows of BPD. We get mired in this all-consuming depression, and feel like the world is collapsing down around us, that nothing was ever good or real or worthwhile, and nothing will ever hold any value to us ever again.

This guide refers to this as "living in the now," or, "living in the moment" because we get into a moment in time and that's all that exists for us. There is no past - we have no recollection of our past abilities to come through tough times, we cannot recall anything that made us feel better in the past, we are unable to pull up former coping techniques.

Likewise, I also notice that sometimes people get stuck in the moment of good times.

While that may not seem like a harmful thing (because who doesn't enjoy feeling good, right?) I think it does more harm than we sometimes allow ourselves to realize.

We are in the moment of good, an almost euphoric moment, and we don't recall the past down times. We don't recognize the cyclic nature of life. We expect and hope and pray that life will always be this euphoric, wonderful, manic.

And it never lasts. Ever.

And when that time euphoria ends, we crash and burn.

I think the key to breaking free of this up-and-down roller coaster ride and genuinely enjoying the good times and having faith that things will get better when we're in the low times, is to break out of the habit or pattern of living in the now.

We need to teach ourselves to learn to recognize the feelings of extreme emotions – mania/euphoria and hopelessness/despair – as manifestations of living in that moment.

We need to learn to stop ourselves in that extended moment and, looking both forward and backward, to give ourselves a reality check.

We need to learn how to feel emotions as they naturally occur rather than grabbing the emotion and surrounding or drowning ourselves in it.

We need to learn how to feel an emotion in its natural state – fleeting, transient – and accept that with open arms.

"And this too shall pass."

The Now – A Double-Edged Sword

I've discussed how the mind in Borderline works when encountering emotional situations. Specifically, I've used the phrase "the now" in relation to depressing moments or tragic times, and explained that a Borderline will feel the sadness, or anger, or betrayal or tragedy and know nothing else. There is no past for the Borderline at that moment. There is no history from which to cull memories of having successfully encountered, dealt with and survived similar moments in their lives. All the Borderline can see in that moment, is that moment. There is no future, nothing can ever change; they can't imagine ever coming through this hard time; there is no recollection or conscious awareness of having come through similar rough spots in the past.

Confusing as it may sound, there really is some recollection of the past. However, it is highly selective. There is a filter in place that will only allow similar tragedies to float to the surface to the Borderline in "the now." They feel their current horror and begin recalling other awful times in their past: a bad breakup, a death in the family, a bad grade, the loss of a pet. The bad instances don't even necessarily have to relate to the actual current situation; instead, the bad events and times serve to reinforce to the Borderline that they are bad, that nothing good ever happens, that these awful things are their fate, that they are merely getting what they so richly deserve. So while the Borderline mind has the ability to rely on personal histories in times of crisis, this is done so only in a limited fashion. We pull out the bits and pieces which serve to justify the negative self-talk tapes we were given, probably at an early age.

The process of recovery teaches the Borderline to recognize when the tape player is on, to turn it off and eventually to record over the negative self-talk with positive, realistic and healthy self-talk.

Another aspect of the double-edged nature of "the now" is when the Borderline tries to look forward while immersed in the horror of the moment. In one sense, we are in "the now" because that moment is all that exists to us and we are unable to clearly see the past. Yet we still, in our own way, will look to the past for consolation, and because we've not yet learned how to see the past clearly, we only see the hurtful fragments.

Likewise, when we look to the future, we don't see clearly. We have our current moment in "the now," which is horrible and excruciating, and we've looked to the past which has shown us only more suffering and agony. Consequently, when we look to the future, all we are able to envision is the hellish existence in which we currently find ourselves.

We find ourselves unable to make plans for the future because we cannot imagine a future in which this tortured feeling doesn't exist. We've justified to ourselves that what we have now is exactly what we've always had so therefore it is what we always will have.

I know there have been times when I've suggested that people live "in the now," and I can see how that could be confusing based on what I've just shared.

There is , I think, a difference between the "Borderline now" and the "real now." The "Borderline now" takes a moment and grabs blindly behind itself for any sort of justification in whatever manner and stretches that horridness across all time – past, present and future – so that the "now" seems to have no beginning, no end and is all-encompassing.

However, the "real now" is a healthy place and is, thankfully, is quite different. A person able to "live in the real now" is:

- One who can feel an emotion without letting it overwhelm them completely;

- One who can look to the past with a positive mental attitude (even in spite of dire present circumstances) and use their past as a frame of reference to provide themselves with the skills and self-encouragement necessary to see them through this time;

- One who can look to the future and see hope, —a light at the end of the tunnel—, formulate a plan to make it through the trying time and is able to see the present as a temporary situation rather than "the end-all-be-all of life as we know it."

The Two Faces of Black-and-White Thinking

While reading the title of this topic, you may be thinking that it's a no-brainer and probably a pretty unimaginative title. However, the "two faces" doesn't necessarily apply to the "black" and the "white" styles of thought. Rather, what I am aiming for is a discussion on the merits – both positive and negative – of the typical Borderline thought processes.

By now, most of us are very aware of the negative aspects of black-and-white, all-or-nothing, love-or-hate, nothing-in-between thinking. We've seen firsthand - at our own hands or at the hands of others - when black-and-white thinking causes problems... at work, with friends, in intimate relationships.

"Well, if you won't do that for me, you must not love me so I hate you!" This is a very generic example of the Borderline's black-and-white thinking and I use the term "thinking" loosely here. Not because I don't believe that Borderlines have the capacity for thought, rather I bring this up because most times, the Borderline doesn't think, or is incapable of thinking or doesn't know how to think when in the midst of a crisis or traumatic moment.

We've discussed triggers before and I've made it clear that including the word "triggers" in subject headings at the discussion board is not required and is even frowned upon. While I recognize that some boards do require this, I've always found that we are unique human beings and we all have different things that "set us off." To ask that a fellow community member or anyone in our daily lives would be able to read our minds, know our inner selves when we don't even know who we are, and ask that they know in advance what may trigger someone is simply asking someone else to take responsibility for our feelings.

The online community [which the author created] is one in which personal responsibility has always been stressed. It is in these moments of crisis the Borderline has a fantastic opportunity to practice, to learn, to heal and to grow. The traditional, as I've pointed out, method of response to many or most situations for the Borderline is to revert to the black-and-white thinking. They feel the most comfortable in the all-or-nothing mentality. They are unable to grasp the concept of grey or of the middle ground.

The very thing that instigates most interpersonal conflict with a Borderline is the very thing that will save the Borderline: the black-and-white thinking. If you have BPD, you may be wondering how this could possibly be a good thing but I'm here to tell you that it's probably the strongest asset you have in your fight for a healthier self.

One of the goals of recovery is to get the Borderline to a place where they are able to deal with problems, moments of crisis and/or trauma in a healthy, reasonable and responsible way. What better way to do this than to ask the Borderline to modify their already strong tendency toward black-and-white, right-or-wrong and funnel these energies into honing their problem solving skills?

While we've been talking about black-and-white as equating to any of the following:

- right-or-wrong
- up-or-down
- love-or-hate
- in-or-out
- good-or-bad
- yes-or-no
- all-or-nothing
- euphoric-or-despondent

the truth is that in problem solving, black-and-white is a useful tool. "If this, then that." It is simple logic.

"If I scream and yell, then they will fire me."

"If I retain composure, then I can work to remedy the situation."

However, this is a moot point if you are unable to recognize your own black-and-white thinking. Why would you feel a need to change something you don't recognize as being wrong?

Many Borderlines have asked me "How do I learn to see the black-and-white?" My answer is to be on the lookout for specific types of words in their thoughts or speech:

- Never
- Always
- Can't
- Hate
- Love
- Horrible
- Wonderful
- Perfect
- Worst

Yes, the word 'love' is in there because it can indeed be a "white" (of the black-and-white thinking variety) feeling that isn't necessarily grounded in reality.

One of the most useful tools in helping the Borderline mind to modify its black-and-white thinking once you are aware of it is to use the Five Steps. The steps are a wonderful black-and-white way for you to address the feelings of crisis during your initial steps into recovery, and will become the foundation of your recovered life. Over time, you will be able to embrace the grey in the world around you and the Five Steps will become second-nature to them.

I do not purport that the Five Steps are the only tool necessary to achieve a healthy, happy life; however, I do find that they are a very effective tool to gain significant progress (with practice) which uses your own innate tendencies to a positive advantage. I have personally found the Five Steps to be a life-savers – literally. I enjoy that the Steps take a long-engrained personality characteristic which has universally been treated like the Black Plague and make subtle modifications which change the entire perspective of the same personality characteristic, from negative to positive using the individual's own self for the metamorphosis.

Homework

Think about some times in your past when you've been caught in that "now" which has had the compounding effect – where a single event has brought about an entire avalanche of negativity from your entire life's history.

Spend some time separating those negative events into separate instances.

As an adult, looking back on any of those events, find the positive that came from the situation(s.) Maybe you met someone new, got a new job offer, saved yourself a lot of money, etc.

Are you able to recognize your own black-and-white thinking? It doesn't have to be present tense recognition. If you're only able to point to incidents from your past as representations of your black-and-white thinking, that's perfectly okay. Being able to recognize it in yourself – presently or in retrospect – is the first step to solving the "problem" of how to start thinking in shades of grey.

Under what circumstances could black-and-white thinking help you? How/when could this way of thinking help others?

144 Putting The Pieces Together

Self-Harm, Past Trauma, Dissociating & Communication

Self-Harm

This is a tough section for me to write because my own personal versions of self-harm were mild in comparison to many peoples. The extent of my self-harm was generally limited to non-scarring acts such as hitting myself with my fists or pulling my hair. I know that many people often struggle with more serious aspects of self-harm such as cutting, or picking, or even swallowing toxic substances or smashing bones with a hammer.

I believe that there are a couple of different reasons that people engage in self-harm:

- To self-punish

- To initiate dissociation

- To attempt to reconnect to the physical sensations of the body(to break out of a dissociative state)

- To seek attention as a cry for help in dealing with the underlying emotional issues

- To escape the underlying emotional issues.

Over the years, as I've spoken to many people who self-harm on a regular basis, all of these reasons came up – whether or not the individual was able to express them in so many words.

My personal forms of self-harm were that of self-punishment. My incidents were always precipitated by a failure of some sort: a verbal fight in a relationship that meant a lot to me, an inability to perform an action (such as a martial arts move) or being told I had done something wrong or inappropriate. I had my old tapes playing that were telling me I didn't deserve happiness and that I needed to be punished. Since I didn't trust those around me to agree with the words on those old tapes, it fell to me to hand out the punishment. And I did. It was generally in the midst of a sobbing fit, or in the middle of a fit of rage.

Once I was able to identify when those tapes were playing, I was better able to work on reprogramming them. I was also able, after a while of work with my recovery tools, to incorporate the Five Steps into my daily life. When a situation presented itself where I felt like I had failed, I continued to list "punish myself" as one of my possible courses of action. It was the ability to list a comfortable known option amongst the unfamiliar, unknown – and therefore, scary – options that allowed me to see that I did indeed have choices beyond self-harm.

It seems to me that the other four underlying reasons for self-harm are all related to being able to deal effectively with emotional issues. While this might seem like common knowledge to some people, if this common theme had not yet occurred to you, I encourage you to spend some time meditating on it. If meditation is not your "thing," please simply allow the concept to float around in your subconscious for a while.

The vast majority of the people I've spoken with who are in the very early stages of recovery from Borderline have a common refrain: "I just can't help myself. I don't want to do it but I can't seem to stop myself." If this rings true for you, I strongly encourage you to give yourself some leeway and flexibility as you tackle this part of your journey. For a long time, self-harm has been your primary way of coping with difficult emotional issues. Because you've merged a physical action with an emotional response in such a dramatic way (blood, scarring, broken bones, violent illness), it will naturally take more work, time, patience, practice and self-forgiveness to break that bond between the physical and emotional.

You've made it this far into the book and you've covered a lot of material – all of which will be helpful to you in overcoming this issue – but please don't expect that you'll suddenly be self-harm-free by the end of the book! It doesn't happen that way. Having the coping techniques at your disposal – the Four Agreements, the Five Steps, understanding of the separation of stuff and the ability to recognize old tapes – will aid you a great deal in being able to better cope with those emotional issues.

Don't expect perfection right off the bat. That's simply setting yourself up for failure. Rather, expect that you will stumble from time to time. Understand this:

It's not about how many times you fall down. It's about how many times you get back up!

Past Trauma

This Past trauma can be anything from repeated sexual abuse to merciless playground teasing; from abandonment through adoption to a nasty relationship break-up. There are, apparently, some in the mental health professional community which operate under the understanding that Borderline Personality Disorder is the same as Post Traumatic Stress Disorder (PTSD). While I don't subscribe to that theory, PTSD can certainly be found co-morbid with BPD in a fairly large segment of the Borderline population.

The methods I advocate in this book to deal with Borderline issues are such that we don't look back to the past; rather, we look to the future and determine for ourselves how we can better deal with current life situations. We also focus on forgiveness but for certain issues – early and prolonged child sexual molestation, rape, repeated physical abuse, torture – a professional is certainly your best bet.

I don't profess to hold all the answers and since I don't categorize myself as someone who's endured past traumas, I don't believe I'm the best person to speak to on the issue of dealing with these issues in a healthy and effective way. I don't even know whether or not it's possible to find a therapist who can help you come to terms with the past traumas, help you work through the PTSD issues and concurrently help you achieve "recovery" from Borderline. Because I believe the issues are different – dealing with flashbacks from old traumas, and focusing on the future in a healthy way – you may need additional care from a team of mental health professionals.

I won't try to gloss over the impact that past traumatic events can have on a person. I think it is important that these issues are dealt with, in a professional and healthy way. I also don't think that the techniques offered in this book will necessarily be the answer. While they may help to a certain degree, I cannot stress enough the importance of having real interactions with a mental health professional about the underlying issues and secondary emotions as a result of those events.

Dissociation

People often wonder what dissociating means. I wish I could give you a clear answer, like "dissociating is like jumping into an ice cold lake in February in Fargo, North Dakota." It doesn't work that way, unfortunately. Dissociation can be explained in as many different ways as there are people who've experienced dissociation because it's a unique experience.

Based on the conversations I've had with many people who've experienced dissociation, the common factor seems to be "overload" when it comes to reasons dissociative states begin. The top reason for overload seems to be emotional in origin. That is to say, when life seems to be piling up and there aren't enough healthy coping mechanisms, the mind begins to shut down and to drown out the external stimuli in order to be able to deal with the information it has already received.

In simple terms, dissociation is dis-associating from your self; distancing your thinking mind from your emotional center. Some people describe it as floating outside of your body. Others say that nothing feels real any more, that they know things are happening in real time and that they're part of the functioning world, but they're not really participating. One woman described it as watching a play but being unsure as to whether she was an actress or part of the audience. Overall, it seems that dissociation is a lack of feeling but still acting on impulse without conscious awareness of thought.

As you become more well-versed in working the Five Steps and become more and more aware of things as they happen, you'll be more likely to be able to nip each issue in the bud rather than allowing them all to "gang up" on you, thus triggering the dissociation. Since dissociation is one of those things that's not easily defined and is experienced differently by each person, it is that much more difficult to provide a clear path to overcoming it. What I do feel comfortable telling you is this: as you do work to integrate the various aspects of your genuine self and learn healthy coping techniques, the need or desire to cope by detaching from yourself will disappear. Of course, I have no clinical substantiation for this claim nor can I say for any certainty that it will happen this way for you. All I can do is share my own experience – as I no longer dissociate – and those of some of the people I've had the opportunity and honor to observe as they progress through their own journey to healthy, happy living.

Author notes:

As I made progress in my own journey toward recovery, I began to see dissociation as a blessing rather than a curse. I began to make connections between the physical sensations – detaching, floating, surreal – to the fact that something was going on inside of me. I allowed that feeling to just be. I continued to try to function as well as I could – I'd still go to work, go through the motions and try to limit myself from doing anything overly-rash or inappropriate. I felt very zombie-like and, at the beginning of my work on dealing with dissociation, I was generally unaware of what it was that was triggering the events. By allowing the feelings to just happen and be, I allowed my subconscious to fiddle with the problem. Sure enough, within a day or two, sometimes as quickly as a few hours, the source of the fugue would become apparent to me. By being able to finally pinpoint what it was that was simmering in my subconscious, I was then able to focus on how to "fix" the problem. I could then work the Five Steps and take an active role in resolving the issue.

Communication

Communication is pretty simple, right? I mean, we all do it, every day. We talk to people, we listen to people, and we share our lives. Communication is something that I think we, as a society, take for granted. We're constantly bombarded with messages – on the radio, in the newspapers, on television, at home, at the office, alongside the highways – but how much of it do we really absorb? Very little, I'd wager.

Communication is so essential to the recovery process that I'm at a loss for words to convey how truly important it really is. You will be called on to communicate with your therapist, your psychiatrist, your support system, your role models and, most importantly, yourself. These communications need to be honest or else you may as well save your energy and not say a single word.

I've encountered many folks who freely admit they lie to their therapists or that they don't tell the whole truth. I think that is a crying shame. It really is. You're spending your money and time to get help from this person and you're not able to be honest? If they don't know what's going on in your life, in your head and heart, how can you possibly expect them to help you?

A lot of folks tell me they keep quiet out of fear of making a poor impression. I'd like to share something with you that actually happened during my first session with Sharon. She asked me, as part of her diagnostic phase, if I'd ever heard voices of people who weren't there. I told her that I had but it was during a time of my life when I wasn't sleeping very well and since then, I'd not "heard voices" again. The topic was never brought up again and I wasn't institutionalized. It was episodic in nature and it was, for my particular situation, mild in comparison to experiences of other people. As a matter of fact, there isn't a month that goes by at the online discussion board where someone doesn't post about their auditory or visual hallucinations. It seems that they are generally related to medication side-effects. The point is, if I, as a layperson, hear about all sorts of "strange" tales, just imagine what a seasoned mental health professional has heard!

Do not be afraid to share your inner thoughts with the right people. By "the right people" I mean that you should be judicious in whom you share things with, but when you select those people, be honest. There's no need to tell your dry cleaner that you occasionally have suicidal thoughts, but a therapist is someone who should hear that because it's important that they know what you're thinking and feeling so they can help you work through it.

A lot of folks are hesitant to bring up that S-word in therapy because they fear a psychiatric lock-up. I want you to know that there is a difference between "I want to kill myself right now and this is how I plan to do it," and "I wanted to die because the whole situation hurt so much." A therapist worth his or her salt would be able to see that the second statement was an expression of pain and frustration at an inability to cope with pain in a healthier way, rather than an explicitly stated imminent threat of harm to self. It's entirely okay to discuss suicidal thoughts with your therapist.

Heck, even well into recovery, it's okay to have suicidal thoughts! More often than not, they are fleeting thoughts that don't take the time to stick around. Once you're into your journey of recovery and can effectively weigh your options, the odds are pretty good that your fleeting thought of suicide as a solution will be dismissed outright. You'll know that there are other ways to cope with pain, anger, sadness or frustration. You will no longer need to consider a permanent solution to a temporary problem. And it's okay to bring this up with your therapist. It's a point of pride that you're able to allow the concept of suicide to enter your mind, and then be able to find alternate solutions on your own!

The last thing I wanted to bring up on the topic of communication is the style in which you communicate.

You can catch more flies with honey than you can with vinegar.

Back in my days of hanging out in an online chat room, there were frequent debates which often got heated. On one subject in particular, I would consistently voice a dissenting point of view. One other participant echoed the sentiment but did so in a very different style. My words were accepted with respect while his words were met with stiff resistance. It's perfectly okay to have a dissenting opinion, but it is also important to recognize that you "get what you give." If you present your opinion with an "in your face" attitude and complete disregard for the opinions of other people, that's what you'll get in return. They'll get back in your face and totally disregard the opinion you just put forth. Respect and courtesy are both a two-way streets.

Back in Chapter Eleven, we talked about boundaries – both giving them and receiving them. I would like to reiterate how important communication is to this process. One of the more difficult things I found personally, and have seen play out for countless others, is the ability to sit with silence in boundary discussions. More often than note, the desire is to spew out a ton of words at the other person as we try to give a boundary and we end up over-explaining ourselves.

Less is more.

If you ask a question, allow the other person the courtesy of hearing, understanding, absorbing and processing your question, and give them the time necessary for them to be able to formulate the response they'd like to give in return.

152 Putting The Pieces Together

> **Poor Communication:** So what do you think? Are you interested in this project? I think this would be wonderful because of A, B and C but I can understand if you have a problem with B and C so we can talk about that later, but I really think this will be fantastic. Are you on-board? How soon do you think we can sign the paperwork and get this thing started?
>
> **Good Communication:** Based on what we've heard, what are your thoughts?

In the first example, the enthusiasm is apparent but the verbal barrage is overwhelming. Four questions are asked all at once and several assumptions have been made. That first example is contrary to many of the principles set forth in this book. Can you list them?

There are several benefits to the second example. The first is that you haven't overwhelmed the person to whom you're speaking. The second is that you've made no assumptions about their thoughts. The third is that you're allowing them the time to process your question and formulate an answer before you move forward. The fourth, and in my opinion, the most important, is that your subsequent questions still have the flexibility of adjustment based on the response you get to this first question. You're taking things one step at a time. Perhaps, even if you thought all the things listed in the first example, the person expressed concerns over A and B rather than B and C. You've managed to "save face" by not making incorrect assumptions, and you do not have to be corrected.

Homework

- If you engage in self-harm, what are some things you have under your control that would help you refrain from acting in an unhealthy manner and, instead, opt for a healthier coping technique?

- Will you aim for a period of time of being self-injury free?

- Will you join a support group?

- If you have not yet spoken of this issue with your support system, how could you bring it up so that you're getting the support that is essential to making such a lifestyle change?

Self-Harm, Past Trauma, Dissociating & Communication 153

- If you've experienced past trauma, pick a two week period of time to observe how that past trauma is currently influencing your life.

    – Are you hearing old tapes?

    – Are you living in fear?

- Are you still harboring anger and/or resentment toward the perpetrator of that trauma but lashing out at anyone nearby in lieu of the actual perpetrator?

- Devise a plan to overcome these issues. Involve as many people as necessary – psychiatrist, therapist, support system – and make it a top priority to achieve your goal.

- If you experience dissociation, get a fresh notebook or start a new file on your computer to track your episodes. Write down how you were feeling, what was going on, what you did during your dissociative episode and how you feel afterward.

- If you're working with a therapist and/or a psychiatrist, share this journal with them.

- Together, determine if your dissociative episodes are biologically based – maybe as a side effect of a medication – or if they're brought on by emotional factors – such as times of extreme stress.

- As part of your efforts to become more effective at setting boundaries and becoming impeccable with your words, practice saying some boundaries. Practice in the mirror, maintaining eye contact with yourself.

- Get accustomed to saying a statement and then waiting.

- Teach yourself to say "I'd like some time to think about that before I respond."

- Carry on mock conversations with yourself from time to time, especially as you prepare to have a difficult discussion with a particular person, so that you feel comfortable saying the words you know to be healthy.

154 Putting The Pieces Together

The Genuine Self

What is your genuine self? This question most often throws people with Borderline for a loop, and they are unable to draw anything but a blank. Are you able to easily identify core aspects of who you are? Most likely, you are confused about your genuine self, as most people afflicted with Borderline are. In this section, we will discuss some of what it takes to determine your personal journey to your genuine self. "what is your genuine self?"

Another way to look at this is by picturing a mirrorball, as the kind you would find at a disco. Picture yourself as the mirrorball with all these tiny little fragments. Maybe when the mirrorball gets pulled from its shipping box, it doesn't look spectacular. Maybe it might even look a little plain or dull. As the saying goes, "no man is an island" and the mirrorball isn't alone for long. Then the lights come on and the mirrorball begins to twirl around slowly. As it does this, different colored lights shine upon the mirrorball.

As we face a particular situation in which we might act the consummate professional, but yet when we face a bill collector or a telemarketer in our personal lives, we might get really angry and start yelling at the person on the other end of the phone. The Borderline often has difficulty determining which aspect is the real them and when they can't, they make the determination that none of them are real and that there is nothing inside of themselves, they're a fraud.

Yet, when we face a crisis at work, it's like the blue light shining on the one particular segment of the mirrorball. When the telemarketer or bill collector catches us at a bad time, it's perhaps the red light now shining on a different section of the mirrorball. All of the pieces of the mirrorball are valuable, and needed and worthwhile. All of them serve to create the whole – the mirrorball. Every fragment of your personality, your "self," serves to create the whole of your genuine self.

The genuine self is going to look and feel different for every single person, but the one thing that all will have in common is that the genuine self is the recovered self. It is By creating and accepting the genuine self, that we become functional, healthy adults capable of facing life's hurdles.

The genuine self is also known, in some circles, as the core self or the core personality. In other words, what is it that you believe?

What are your views on politics?

On religion?

On corporal punishment?

On capital punishment?

On abortion?

On censorship?

On personal freedom?

On homosexuality?

I don't suggest that you need to answer these questions and then you'll be "cured" of Borderline. I pose these questions as a way to get you to think about what you believe. We spoke in Chapter Seven of mirroring. I wouldn't be surprised if your answers to some or all of these questions are "I don't know" or "I'm not sure." I would also expect to hear "It depends on the situation" and that's a fantastic response – provided the situation is based on the topic rather than the person with whom you're discussing the topic.

> *If you don't know what you stand for, you'll stand for anything.*

Let's use the subject of abortion as an example. If your stance on abortion depends on the health of the mother and/or the circumstances under which the fetus was conceived, I would accept your response of "It depends on the situation" as a healthy response because it is externally situation-specific.

If, however, you were inclined to believe that abortion was wrong under most circumstances but okay if the conception was the product of a rape. Let's further say that you got into a debate with a specific individual who was able to undermine your argument. As your blood pressure goes through the roof, you may become angry at this particular person, causing you to suddenly become "absolutely, 100%, without exception pro-choice." I would then reject your response of "It depends on the situation." In this case, you've allowed your position or belief to change or be modified based on an emotional reaction to a specific and direct challenge. It has become internalized and is no longer based on theory. Your altered position is based on the person with whom you're discussing the topic rather than the situation itself. You've modified your belief because of an opposing argument, while the theoretical situation has remained unchanged. It is the shifting beliefs based on shifting internal emotions that is unhealthy. Keeping an open mind while holding on to your own beliefs is healthy. Facing these moments of duality gives you a tremendous frame of reference for understanding the grey in life.

And yet, I still tell you to keep your mind open to opposing points of view. If I'm telling you to hold fast to your beliefs but turn around and tell you to be open to the views of others, how can I be right in both cases? If the answer to one question is black and the answer to a similar question is white, which one is right? The answer is: both are right. The answer to both is grey. The moment you can see and understand that enigma, the rest will fall into place naturally. You'll suddenly have this tremendous frame of reference for understanding grey. This moment will be your own light bulb. As you work through some of life's larger issues and get a grasp of what it is that you truly believe, you'll be faced with these moments of duality more and more frequently. My personal light bulb issue was trying to reconcile "pro-choice" with "no capital punishment."

Your genuine self will be unique to you. You may share similarities with some folks and be extremely dissimilar to other folks, and yet, both groups of people can be your friends. When you've solidified your genuine self, you'll be able to recognize that everyone else around you also has a genuine self and no two people need to be the exact same. People need not share the same thoughts, beliefs or opinions on any subject, let alone all of them. By embracing your own genuine self, you'll suddenly be free to embrace the genuine selves of those around you because they will no longer represent a lot of work – you no longer need to change them or convert them to your way of thinking. You'll be content to allow them to be exactly who they are while you continue being exactly who you are. And if, or should I say, when you encounter someone who wants you to change, you'll weigh their request against your genuine self, work the Five Steps, apply the Four Agreements and be able to determine whether or not that aspect of yourself is open to change or not. Sometimes these scenarios might mean that a particular person will chose to avoid you because of your refusal to bend to their wishes, and your genuine self will be okay with that. You'll know that their boundary was unhealthy and that it's probably best to end the association with that person.

The genuine self is really a remarkable sense of inner peace and tranquility. It doesn't mean that you've earned a pass into Nirvana or Utopia. Nor does it mean that life will be a constant state of "smooth sailing." There will still be upheavals, fights, moments of extremes – that's part of life and it cannot be changed. With the solidity and security of the genuine self, though, you will be able to weather those ups and downs with the calm and peaceful understanding that, no matter what, you will conduct yourself in accordance with the beliefs of your genuine self.

You'll be comfortable knowing that you can be a Parent or a Student or an Employee or a Spouse at any given time, depending on what the situation calls for without losing your core, genuine self and set of beliefs. Putting on the appropriate "hat" for the situation doesn't change your genuine self.

The genuine self isn't necessarily an entirely new person or persona. Picture, if you will, a hunk of clay. Over time, that clay has been molded into a square, a circle, smushed into some semblance of an ashtray, reformed into a puppy dog, a tree, a flower and a rolling pin. The clay is still the same clay but each time, it has looked like something different. The goal of getting to the genuine self is to settle on a particular shape or design – that reflects who you are at your very core – and put it into the kiln to harden so that it is no longer malleable. This is your opportunity to become the person you were always meant to become.

Homework

- How do you feel about what you've read in this section?

- What do you envision your life will be like when you've gotten yourself to the point where you're comfortable with your genuine self?

- Having read all the material in this book, how confident are you that recovery is possible?

- Pick at least one (but up to three) role model that you can look to as you begin re-assembling your genuine self.

- For a period of two weeks, pay closer attention to the news and current events. Pick an issue or a couple of small issues and try to get a handle on what your stance, position or belief on that subject is. Your first thoughts may require some fine-tuning as you do more research, hear more opinions or events change. That's okay and be sure to give yourself that flexibility.

18 Goal Setting

Now that you have all of this information and have begun working with the coping techniques through the exercises, begun expanding your Learning Library through the homework assignments and have, hopefully, begun to see that it is possible to live a healthy, happy life after a diagnosis of Borderline Personality Disorder, how are you going to go about getting yourself from this point to the point of actually living that healthy, happy life? The key, my friend, is in goal setting.

I've mentioned it several times before: if you expect to read this book and be miraculously cured of BPD, you're setting yourself up for failure. It just won't happen. It will take time, patience, effort, hard work, practice and forgiveness – of yourself and others. We've covered a great number of topics in this book and none of them, in my opinion, are all that easy to absorb and assimilate. They'll require dedication and a formulated plan to achieve.

It is my recommendation that you take two week steps. That is, work on one small thing at a time. Pick one, any one, and focus on that alone for a period of two weeks. I don't mean to imply that you should ignore all of the other things you've learned up to that point. Instead, I want you to tackle this journey of recovery by taking baby steps. As I mentioned earlier in the section where I equated this process to the couch potato who wishes to become a competitive Olympic decathlete, true success is built one segment at a time.

It is important to have goals because they keep us aiming for an end result. If we have no goals, how will we know when we've achieved them? When you first heard the term Borderline Personality Disorder, your first goal was probably to "get better." That's a noble goal – and certainly achievable – but it's very vague and doesn't offer you any milestones by which you could measure your success and progress.

162 Putting The Pieces Together

The goal of this chapter is to help you in learning effective goal setting procedures so that you can successfully complete your journey toward healthy, happy living.

Goals should be achievable.

There's nothing worse or more self-esteem crushing than setting to set yourself up for failure. Make sure your goals are achievable so that you can mark something off your list and revel in that sense of accomplishment. Once again, let's look at some examples of unachievable goals and then correct them.

Ineffective Goals

1. I want to get better.
2. I want to pass my drivers test.
3. I want to lose a bunch of weight.
4. I want a better job.
5. I don't want to be such a freak anymore.

Effective Goals

1. I want to be able to maintain a professional cool when in meetings I consider to be a waste of time.
2. In order to pass my drivers test, I need to take a Drivers Education course and study the materials by the test date next month.
3. In order to lose fifty pounds in six months, I need to eat 500 calories per day less and exercise 500 calories per day more than I do right now.
4. In order to be happier during my work hours, I need to find a job that will afford me the freedom to express my creativity, will be flexible with the working hours and is in closer proximity to my home and this will require an updated resume, regular searching of the various places ads are placed as well as research on the companies and improvement of my interviewing skills.
5. Since I have so many areas in which I feel freakish, my first step will be to begin identifying those situations so that I can work the Five Steps and incorporate my other coping techniques to eventually eliminate these feelings. While the list will be ongoing, the first draft should be completed by next Saturday.

One of the worst things you could do is set yourself a "negative goal." The subconscious understands only first person positive statements. The subconscious, for instance, will ignore an affirmation or goal of "I want to quit smoking" or, as shown above, "I don't want to be a freak." Instead, rephrase your goals and/or affirmations in positive terms: "I am smoke-free" or "My goal is to be a former smoker." By keeping things positive, you're over-writing the old tapes of negativity and helping your subconscious to help you in your journey toward health and recovery.

Goals should be measurable.

Even if you make your goal something simple like "I want to go as long as I can self-harm-free," that is a measurable goal because you can measure that in hours and days, hopefully in weeks, months and years. In the previous examples of effective goals, the second goal was clearly defined and easily measurable: there was a measurable time-frame of six months and there were definite food and exercise goals embedded within the larger goal.

Let's expand on the weight loss goal. The basic premise in the initial and ineffective goal is that you know how much you currently weigh and that you'll know when you've hit the "bunch of weight" mark. Furthermore, the mini-goals in the effective example indicate that you'll need to know how much you're currently eating, know how much 500 calories worth of food represents as well as how many calories you'll be burning. If you stuck with the first goal and didn't have a scale, didn't know how much exercise you were doing or the nutritional value of the foods you were consuming, how would you know how close you were to achieving your goal – let alone know if you were headed in the right direction?

If you were to proceed on the effective goal, the mini-goals – of food and exercise – would guide you toward the larger goal – losing 50 lbs in 6 months. Both of the mini-goals can be worked on concurrently – at the same time. You can do research on nutrition values, you can find any of the number of websites that provide "activity to calories burned" conversions, you can join a gym or purchase a piece of equipment that will track the calories burned for you, such as a heart rate monitor.

A pound is 3,500 calories. By reducing your intake by 500 cals per day and increasing your output by 500 cals per day, that's a net effect of 7,000 cals, or 2 lbs per week, lost.

Goals should be flexible.

Remember that we discussed, in the Five Steps, that nothing is carved in stone and the more room for flexibility you build into your plans, the less likely you are to be flustered, tempted to quit or get angry that things didn't happen in the timeframe or in the manner you expected. There's that word again: expectations. Remember that if things don't turn out as you would have hoped, you are free to examine your options again. You might find that you should adjust your goals, lengthen the timetable and/or add mini-goals that will assist you in achieving that larger goal.

Flexibility is one of those "grey" things that people who are accustomed to thinking and acting in a world filled with black-and-white find uncomfortable. If the mini-goal is not met, they reason, then the entire goal is unachievable and the entire project should be scrapped.

Getting back to that weight loss goal, what happens when it's your brother's birthday or your co-worker's baby shower? If you drink too much beer, scarf down too many chips, eat too much cake, have too much punch and don't make it to the gym that day, is the entire goal worth tossing out the window? Not likely. The physical body is runs on the law of averages when it comes to weight management. One really good day or one really bad day won't make or break the goal. Again:

It's not about how many times you fall down. It's about how many times you get back up!

Goals should be accountable.

Looking at the goal pertaining to professionalism in time-wasting meetings, how will you measure that? Remember, that Borderline has skewed or twisted most of our thinking and perceptions, especially with respect to our own behavior. Do you think it wise to rely solely on your own perceptions as to your improvement in the board room?

I realize how scary a concept it is to share your goals with other people. There is the fear that they will laugh at your goals, that they will try to undermine you and, a whole myriad of Borderline conjectures can crop up when we are faced with the possibility of sharing a piece of ourselves with other people.

I don't ask that you rent a full-size billboard on the side of the highway in the middle of the city to announce your goals. This is when your support system comes into play. If you're trying to lose weight, find an exercise buddy or join a support group – online or in real life, with face-to-face meetings. If you want to improve your professionalism, find a mentor or role model in those meetings so that you can get honest feedback. You needn't tell anyone that you're working to overcome Borderline Personality Disorder; you can simply mention that you find the meetings a colossal waste of time and you're afraid of how your attitude might be portraying itself – would they mind giving you some feedback and constructive criticism on how you might better mask your annoyance.

Without external accountability, it's a whole lot easier for you to welsh on your commitments to your goals. The purpose of the goal setting process is for you to succeed in your goals so it's imperative that you give yourself every possible advantage when you set out to achieve something. External accountability will also provide you with encouragement, which and that is often a wonderful thing, especially when you get frustrated, fall behind schedule or are tempted to give up on your goals. The more support you have, the more likely you are to succeed.

It takes a village to raise a child.

No, I'm not calling you a child. I'm saying that there is a lot of material to be read, understood, absorbed, practiced and incorporated. You're only human and you needn't and shouldn't do it alone. You are NOT alone!

Homework

- Pick three things you want to work on. Write large goals for those three things. Then define some mini-goals that will help you achieve those large goals. Now review them:
- Are they positive in nature? Are they effective?
- Are they accountable?
- Are they measurable?
- Are they flexible?

- Who will be your support system in achieving these goals? How will you broach the subject with these people?

- Describe your feelings, thoughts, hesitations, and fears about setting forth on the journey to achieving these goals. What coping techniques do you have at your disposal to deal with these challenges?

- Get yourself a notebook (or some other tool) to measure your progress as you reach for your goals. Set up a system of rewards as you reach important milestones. Fulfill those rewards!

Coping with Crisis Feelings

In this section, we will take a practical approach to dealing with some of the more common situations that cause us to feel as if we're in a crisis, a no-win situation, a cataclysmic event that will wash over us and will drown us. Are you able to recognize the drama in the preceding sentence? Are you able to recognize the black-and-white that's contained in those simple words? If so, you're on the right track and you've come a long way from when you first picked up this book and certainly a long way since your diagnosis.

I blew up at my significant other. Now what do I do?

Since you probably didn't carry this book with you during the incident with your significant other and you weren't reading along at the time, it's probably a safe assumption that you've removed yourself from the situation. Whether that separation came about with you storming off, your significant other driving away or either one of you hanging up the phone, the time apart right now is what both of you need.

As you have this time apart, you have many options available to you and this means you have a great deal of control over your immediate future. While it might not seem like it, you do indeed have more control than you might be feeling or believing. Take this time to calm yourself as best you can. Do something that soothes you – watch a movie, read some of a book, get on the internet and surf for mindless stuff, go for a brisk walk, practice some deep breathing, meditation or grounding exercises. Right now, it's important to calm yourself down and stop. Stop obsessing over the argument. Stop beating yourself up for acting irrationally. Stop fuming over your significant other's insensitivity or whatever else it was. Just stop.

You do indeed have choices but before you can make a choice, you need to figure out what the problem is. Do you know why you blew up? Do you have a clear and rational understanding of the events that took place? Are you able to understand why your blowing up might not have been a desirable action, especially if you now feel like you made a mistake in doing so?

Every couple has disagreements, arguments and differences of opinion. This is because every person is their own unique self and they are entitled to think, feel and believe whatever they choose. That even includes their right to say and do what they would like at any given time. Simply because your significant other voiced an opinion, or did something that you didn't agree with or took exception to does not mean they hate you, want to break up with you or think that you're a worthless person. Are you able to allow your partner to have his or her opinion? Are you able to recognize that your partner has feelings and may have trouble expressing them? Are you able to acknowledge that two people may get upset with one another and still be able to sustain a relationship?

In most cases of a Borderline blow up, the negative self-talk tapes have been playing underneath the conscious level and while the significant other is saying or doing something that triggers the Borderline thinking, you were probably unaware of the feelings going on inside of you. Perhaps your feelings got hurt or you reverted to black-and-white thinking and your blow up was in "retaliation" for the perceived injustice you felt.

After stopping and taking time to calm yourself, you need to determine the problem at hand. Did your significant other say something about ending the relationship? Did your significant other do or say something that you now realize to be innocuous and don't know what to do next? Do you feel as if your relationship may be in jeopardy? Do you believe that you've committed an unforgivable act?

These are all feelings. They are probably not the problem. The problem might be that you feel you acted out and want to make amends and don't know how. The problem might be that you are still angry but you don't know what to do next without further jeopardizing the relationship.

Coping with Crisis Feelings   169

So what things could you do to address the problem, rather than the feelings? Perhaps you could offer a heartfelt apology and explain to your significant other what it was that set you off and how you plan to work on preventing future blow ups. Perhaps you could wait for your significant other to come speak with you when they feel ready or safe in approaching you. Perhaps you could journal for a while until you come to a more clear understanding of why you did what you did, and why you're still angry before approaching your significant other. The key here is to come up with at least three possible courses of action. This is the process of working the Five Steps.

In order to reach the point where you're able to devise the three possible courses of action, you need to focus on what happened and why it happened. You need to put on your objective hat and apply all that you've learned in this book to the situation that just occurred. It will be in retrospect and that's okay. You're learning. You're not expected to be the Olympic Decathlete on the first try. Or even the first twenty tries. Working in retrospect is perfectly fine for right now.

So how will you know which course of action to choose? That will be up to you entirely. It is your relationship, your life, your choice. It's not something that can be decided for you through a book written by someone who doesn't know you, your situation or your relationship. It's not even a decision that can be made by a close friend who does know you, your situation and your relationship. This is where you need to take responsibility for your actions and make a decision – a smart, calm, rational decision based on the Five Steps rather than on Borderline thinking.

Please remember that nothing is ever final. Many people worry a great deal about making the "wrong" decision when it comes to relationship issues. Relationships are pliable, fluid things; they are not granite or a precious diamond that will become worthless with an inappropriate tap of the chisel. If you make a decision that does not work out for the best, you can't undo it and that's what scares a vast majority of folks. Once things get to a certain point where you believe that you made perhaps an unwise decision, you have a new problem at hand. So you work the Five Steps again and make a more informed decision at that time.

Don't forget. The most important part of all of this is to DO IT! Whatever you've determined to be your best course of action to solving the problem that resulted from the blow up at your significant other, it won't happen and won't affect change unless you take action and actually do it.

As scary a concept as it is, trust and honesty are probably the "magic keys" to unlocking the secrets of a relationship. When speaking with your significant other, if you trust and speak candidly, the odds are usually much more in your favor to obtaining a reconciliation. Whether your words are "I'm scared of losing you," or "I get so overwhelmed and I don't yet know how to react so I lash out" or "I get angry and I don't yet know how to express that without blowing up," you'll find that your partner is more receptive to hearing what you have to say when you are completely truthful with them. So many times, Borderlines speak out of hurt and anger and say some pretty rotten things to cover up their genuine feelings. By sharing the genuine feelings with your significant other, you'll be acting in one of the healthiest ways possible to ensure a long-lasting and happy relationship. There are no guarantees but the odds are way better!

I feel totally worthless, like a failure, unlovable.

First off: You're not alone. There are countless people right this very moment who feel the same way you do. The hope is in the fact that you're a step ahead of them because you have this book and all of its resources to help you get through this time and these feelings.

Next, you should know that you have every right in the world to feel whatever it is that you're feeling. The genuine you is entitled to feel the feelings as they come to you. Think of yourself as a house with it's windows open on a fine spring day. Suddenly, there is the stench of a skunk's spray drifting into your house. What would you do? Would you hurry up and close all the windows so that the skunk odor stays trapped in the house, suffocating and nauseating you? Or would you leave the windows open and let the skunk-scented breeze drift through and out of your home?

One of the most important things to remember when you're feeling lousy is that feelings are temporary. Don't try to force yourself to feel something that you're not yet ready to feel. Trust that your feelings will change.

Of course I'm going to recommend reviewing the coping techniques discussed in this book and then flipping through the things you've made notes about in your Learning Library and/or journals. Beyond that, though, I want you to recognize that feelings are emotions and not facts. There is a difference between the two. The fact that a chair is blue is just that: a fact. Now, you could have feelings about the chair being blue: it doesn't match the room, it's a hideous shade of blue, it reminds you of the chair you used to have your punishments in as a child, etc. The feelings are different and separate from the fact that the chair is blue.

See if you can talk to the inner voices that are telling you to feel like a failure. Try to counteract them with some of the successes you've experienced in your life. Argue back to the voice that tells you that you're unlovable. Come up with instances where someone else has shown you love, compassion, caring and understanding. Try to immerse yourself in those past feelings. If you can accurately remember what it felt like to be on the receiving end of that person's actions, it's not likely that you felt – at that moment – that you were unlovable. To the contrary, you felt loved and worthy of that love.

I lost my job!

Your job does not define your genuine self. If you lost your job because of something you did or did not do, that is something you can take responsibility for but please don't wallow in that for very long. Look at it as a learning experience and truly try to learn from the experience. Work on becoming more professional or controlling your temper in a work setting. Pick yourself up, dust yourself off and go find a new job. It may be the best thing to ever have happened to you because, while you were at that other job, you were closed to new possibilities and learning experiences.

If you lost your job due to economic factors or corporate restructuring, don't sweat it. This decision was completely impersonal and you should make no assumptions whatsoever about your job performance or your worth as an employee, let alone as a human being. Maybe this is a period of time where you can re-evaluate your options in terms of career goals or financial freedom. Examine how well the job you just lost was suited to your genuine self and perhaps make modifications to your job search. You might be surprised at the new opportunities available to you when you expand your horizons.

I don't like my family!

I hate to be the one to break it to you but there are a lot of us in the world who don't necessarily like our families, or at least sections or specific members of the family. You're not alone and you shouldn't feel guilty for not liking someone. Families are groups of people we are related to through the luck of the genetic draw. We did not choose our family, nor did they choose us – unless, of course, you're adopted like I am. If you are adopted, keep in mind that the decision to "choose" you was made many years ago, when you were an infant or a child. You're entitled to grow, learn and mature and become a very different person than you were twenty or thirty years ago. If the person you've become doesn't like the people they are, so be it.

While no one needs to give you permission to dislike anyone else, I do want to make it clear that you are not under any legal obligation to attend family events. Nor are you required to live your life in accordance with the family norms. You needn't send birthday and anniversary cards if you don't feel like it.

You have the right to say no. Even to family. If a family member asks you to do something that you don't want to do, you have the right to say no. I would hope that you would do it in a respectful manner, though. Remember to be impeccable with your words and allow the other person to have time to assimilate what you've told them before proceeding. Use the Five Steps liberally when dealing with family members you don't care for. While you cannot undo genetics (or lifelong understandings) of who your family is, you can take control over how you deal with and respond to them as individuals. If that means you talk to some members of your family and not others, it means, to me, that you're living a healthy life rather than play-acting that you're the Cleaver family. As a healthy, integrated adult with a solid genuine self, you are entitled to determine with whom you associate, regardless of their tie to you on the family tree.

Remember to set effective boundaries and keep the Four Agreements and Five Steps at the forefront of your mind when dealing with problematic family members.

I'm stuck and don't know what to do!

Whatever the situation might be, my first advice is to work the Five Steps. Give yourself time to deal with the situation. Pull the Four Agreements into the mix when you work Steps Number Two and Three. Remember to separate stuff, where appropriate, and take one small step at a time. Virtually all problems can be broken down to smaller, more manageable problems or challenges. You have a support system for a reason – use it! You are not an island and it is perfectly acceptable for you to reach out to those around you for help and/or advice. Sometimes all we really need is a sounding board. "These are the things I see as my options. This is what my instinct is telling me I should do. What do you think?" Be very aware that you are not running to other people for the answers to your life issues; rather try to come up with solutions on your own and then ask for feedback from people you trust. When someone tells you "this is the answer" you've learned nothing. The whole purpose of this journey has been to learn new things and become self-sufficient. Don't undermine yourself, no matter how strong the urge might be.

174 Putting The Pieces Together

Questions & Answers

Early on in the process of writing this book, I sought input from those around me. I created a special email address and posted a section on the website indicating that people could send in their questions and, time permitted, I would answer as many as I could. Unfortunately, I received literally over one hundred emails per day. That was simply more motivation for me to complete this book because it showed me just how many people had questions about Borderline Personality Disorder. I decided that it would be helpful to have a section in this book devoted entirely to answering "consumer questions" because, after all, you are who this book is for. Keep in mind that some of these questions come from people who care about someone who has been diagnosed with or whom they believe may have Borderline.

If I tell you my life story, along with how I react to some situations, can you tell me if I have Borderline?

Nope. I'm not a licensed therapist and I'm not qualified to make that diagnosis for you. If you're interested in a formal diagnosis, I strongly recommend you seek a mental health professional's opinion. If, however, regardless of label, you would like to work on leading a healthy, happy life, then I think you're taking a positive step. I've met and worked with (in a peer support way) many people who do not have a formal diagnosis, but have committed themselves to finding better ways to cope so that they too can live a healthy, happy life. A label is just a label. If you recognize yourself as you research BPD and want to make some changes, I applaud your decisions but I will not pretend to be able to offer a definitive diagnosis – through an email, over the internet, from a phone call or anything else. I'm just not trained, qualified or licensed to do that!

There are times when I feel powerless to stop myself from doing something destructive (or self-destructive). How do you stop that from happening? I feel paralyzed!

You know, I spent a good number of years of my life living with the feeling of complete powerlessness. I would laugh through the tears of despair because I totally felt that there was nothing – not a damn thing – I could do to take control over my life or myself because the universe was stacked against me. Nothing I ever said, thought, did or believed ever lasted very long. Everything was transient and temporary. Usually it was a self-fulfilling prophecy because I never truly believed that I was capable of making substantial changes in the way I approached the world and my life. But more importantly, I was quite simply ill-equipped to make those changes, the ones I so desperately wanted to happen miraculously. I just didn't know how.

I hate to be the one to have to break this to you but the answer to "how do I stop this from happening" is "you stop it." Now, while that might sound trite and overly simplistic, that's what it boils down to. Granted, there's more to it than just deciding one afternoon to stop doing self-destructive things. It takes practice, patience, forgiveness and a determination to overcome what you have been in the past, to achieve something greater, something more.

I knew about The Five Steps for about two months before I could effectively use them. For the first few therapy sessions following the introduction of The Five Steps, I would sit in the office and cry. I would whine that I knew the basics, I knew the process intellectually but I was powerless to stop the cycle or spiral into the depths of despair which prompted the destructiveness.

The problem was that I believed at that time that intellectual knowledge of a principle or theory should translate into instant application on a regular and daily basis of that same principle or theory. We are human. It doesn't work that way. No matter how much we wish we could be more computer-like and simply plug in new coding, it just isn't that easy for us.

Most of us took several years, even decades, to perfect slide into self-destructiveness; it's more "crazy" than the Borderline itself to think that simply by intellectually understanding a concept that we'll instantly become better, healthier, more well-adjusted individuals. It just can't happen that way.

That said, stopping the destruction and regaining the power to unparalyze oneself is a process of retraining your brain and thought patterns. It takes trial and error. It takes practice and patience and forgiveness of self. It takes determination and grit to pick yourself up one more time and try again to stop the cycle or slide a bit sooner the next time.

What is the impact of Borderline Personality Disorder on children?

First, it should be clearly understood that I am by no means an expert on this subject. I have no children of my own and I have no clinical observation experience with regard to BPD and children. What I offer here is my own insight, thought and belief. Nothing more.

That said, I think it's similar to the cycle of abuse where it simply perpetuates itself. I think that a child exposed to unpredictability and an unhealthy home environment is most likely to believe that such things are normal. As that child ages, he or she will likely emulate the example set at home and/or replay the tapes she heard during childhood, resulting in a continued and similar pattern of Borderline unpredictability.

So does that mean you think the people with Borderline are victims?

To some degree, yes, a person with Borderline is the victim of a disordered personality. They may have even been subjected to a degree of abuse – emotional, verbal, physical and/or sexual – in their past.

Are people with Borderline aware of the pain they inflict onto those around them as a result of their disorder?

Sometimes. And that's not a cop-out. There are times when the thought process is such that we might harbor intense feelings of hurt, anger or hatred which provide a conscious thought process which results in direct action. "You broke up with me; I'll get even with you!"

There are other times when the Borderline thought process is so subtle, so automatic, so deeply ingrained that conscious thought is not there; it's simple reflex. Granted those reflexes were learned and they can be unlearned, but in those instances, there is no awareness of external pain being inflicted on others.

Would you say that people with Borderline should not be held responsible for their harmful actions?

Absolutely not! People with Borderline should indeed be held responsible for their harmful actions. If anything, they should be held to more rigid standards; at least in the beginning of the recovery process.

Why do you say that?

We are all responsible for our actions, regardless of our past. We may not have been able, as small children, to learn healthier ways of coping if none were presented to us during our formative years. But as adults, we are certainly capable of learning "new tricks." In the United States, we hold criminal offenders to different standards based on chronological age. For instance, a child of fourteen would most likely not be tried as an adult. Rather, that child would rightly be classified as a juvenile and we, as a society, commonly hold the belief that children of that age could not know better and, therefore, would and should not be held to the standards of adults, who should know better.

People with Borderline, for the most part, know that something is wrong. They might blame external sources – the dog, the mean teacher, the nasty neighbor, the judge who's holding a grudge – but they still inherently recognize that there are other ways to handle situations. They know that not everyone blows up into a violent rage when confronted with a police officer writing a moving violation ticket. They know that millions of people are faced with unemployment or downsizing and do not suffer ill effects – bankruptcy, foreclosure, etc. – and manage to find a way to achieve continued survival. They recognize that healthier ways of coping exist and because of that awareness, the failure to actively seek to confront life's issues in a one of those healthier ways makes them entirely responsible for their harmful actions. In short, knowing right from wrong and still perpetrating the wrong makes one responsible for the consequences.

One of the hardest things to accept when beginning the journey toward a healthier, happier life beyond Borderline is responsibility and consequence to actions. By allowing any small measure of "Oh, it's okay, don't worry about it, you have Borderline" into the picture, the person with Borderline is instantly enabled to lead a chaotic, Borderline, roller coaster life, devoid of responsibility. If it's "a free pass" in this one instance, then by black-and-white standards, it should be "a free pass" in ALL circumstances.

By holding a person with Borderline to some stringent standards of responsibility and systematically imposing consistent consequences to actions, the person with Borderline is then assisted in the erasure of the old tapes that told them otherwise.

How can you say that? Have you lost all compassion toward people with Borderline? Do you somehow feel superior to those of us that aren't as far along as you?

Not at all. I don't feel superior in the least. The immediately preceding questions and answers were answered during my first six months of recovery-oriented work, while I was still very much "very Borderline." I, of all people, recognize that there is a process to achieve a Borderline-free life and that not everyone will follow the same path. Heck, I doubt if it's possible for ANYONE to follow the same path toward a healthier, happier life as anyone else. I think Borderline and recovery work are very much like snowflakes – no two are alike.

I've been called all sorts of things over the last few years with regard to my work in the Borderline community. I've been called cruel, cold, callous, heartless, unforgiving, uncompassionate, clueless and a slew of other things. I recognize that I'm very much a perfectionistic type of person and I hold myself – and those around me, especially those coming to me for help, assistance and guidance – to very high standards. I don't believe in perfection itself but I do believe in one hundred percent commitment. I believe there are certain things that cannot and should not be sugar-coated. I believe that support without a recovery focus is simply enabling. To sugar-coat or tippy-toe around certain hardcore truths are counterproductive to recovery because the hard lessons do need to be learned. After all, those around people with Borderline regularly refer to feeling as though they need to walk on eggshells. If that's the norm, what purpose does further tip-toeing serve? In order to make an omelet, you've gotta crack a few eggs.

Holding people with Borderline to stringent standards, I believe, is very important during the beginning processes because, in essence, it's "speaking Borderline." Black-and-white thinking is, for the most part, how someone with Borderline views the world. The goal – of healthy, happy living – is to be able to get the Borderline person to see things in varying shades of grey. But initially, when all that can be seen is black or white, handling the person with grey responses does nothing more than add to the confusion and/or chaos. By imposing black or white consequences to actions, the person with Borderline then teaches themselves, in essence, to seek out the grey on their own.

Did you ever have to deal with something like this – the black or white consequences to actions?

You betch-ya! Of course I did. Otherwise, I wouldn't be as emphatic about the whole concept as I am. I speak to it from personal experience. Without black or white consequences, I would not have been able to make progress on my own road to recovery.

By being told up front, "If you do this, then the consequence will be that" I was able to make decisions. I cannot begin to tell you the enormous difference this made in my life, especially after living with an old tape in my head that told me the consequences were constantly changing and I "couldn't win for losing." The world – at least in one small area,: a romantic relationship – finally made sense. My life and the universe no longer resembled a Salvador Dali painting, with everything melting together, barely recognizable from its original form. I suddenly had a frame of reference. "If this, then that."

Don't get me wrong: it took quite a few attempts to fully understand and incorporate this concept into my regular, daily life. At first, I didn't trust the "then that" portion. I listened to the old tape in my head that said, "Yeah, he might say 'then that' but he'll change that on me" or "I can get him to change 'then that' into 'then this' and I can skate by." I didn't trust that I really had control over my fate or the outcome of a situation.

Also, it took me several tries to be able to catch myself in time to remember that there were these black or white consequences to my actions. If I screamed my fool head off at this guy, he'd tell me to go home. Well, I might not remember that consequence until I was three sentences into screaming. But by being able to scream, "Yeah, I know – you're going to send me home because I'm screaming and I'm sorry for that but I just don't know how else to handle things right now" I was at least showing honesty. Honesty in communication in interpersonal communication. – Wow, what a concept.

I don't think I can bring myself to be that honest to another person. Is there any other way around it? Something else I can do?

If there is, I don't know what it might be. Honesty works wonders. (More on this later.)

But it would make me so open and vulnerable. I don't think I can do it!

Whether you think that you can or whether you think that you cannot, you are right. Thoughts are things and to change the things you do, you must first change your thoughts. This is another variation on erasing the old tapes and re-recording new tapes that tell you healthier ways to cope with situations.

What was it like to be on the receiving end of "consequences to actions" from an emotional, rather than intellectual, perspective?

Ooh, it was rough. But only at the beginning. I hated being given direct, clear consequences. It felt like the end of the world. Each time was catastrophic. Every consequence was cataclysmic. If my boyfriend (at the time) told me that he didn't like being around me when I was an emotional wreck and he wanted me to leave, and that I could come back when I was better able to conduct myself in an adult, rational manner, I flipped out.

My whole life and my entire belief system revolved around the old tapes that said "all sickness is death" and I firmly believed, in my skewed Borderline way, that any slight – no matter how insignificant – was a direct reflection on my value and worth as a human being. If a friend cancelled plans, it was because I was a rotten person. If I said no to someone, I would be dumped, rejected or abandoned. Because of this inherent – and largely subconscious – thought process and sub-basement level self-esteem, I often acted on the premise that any rejection of behavior meant a complete rejection of me as a person.

It took many repetitions of this enforcement of consequence for me to fully understand that behavior was separate from worthiness, lovability and value as a person. And those first few moments of consequence enforcement felt – truly – like my world was ending.

You've spoken about reaction versus response. What do you mean by that?

Reactions exist on a visceral level. They are akin to the prehistoric "fight or flight" question hard-wired in the human body. A reaction is internal.

A response, on the other hand, is the external representation to the outside world as a direct result of the cognitive ability to accept input, weigh options, select an appropriate one and act on that decision.

What does this distinction have to do with recovery from Borderline? Why is it so important?

People with Borderline live their lives primarily on reactions. "If this, then that." If they get hurt or perceive a threat of hurt, they react with defense mechanisms. The reaction is automatic, no thought involved. There is no reason, rationale or logical thought. There is no analysis of fact or examination of probable outcome based on possible courses of action.

Recovery from Borderline brings about the awareness of the ability to operate on a response level. The Five Steps, for example, afford an individual the opportunity to feel the reaction, examine it, come up with possible responses, determine the most appropriate one at the time and then act accordingly.

This process, in and of itself, is the essence of healthy, happy living. Without being able to recognize the distinction between reaction and response, a person will not be able to achieve healthy, happy living. They will merely continue living in a world of instant reactions without conscious thought or awareness of the consequences their actions will likely bring about.

When the person in my life with Borderline paints me "black" and shuts me out, is it a punitive action or a coping mechanism?

Without being able to speak in absolute certainty, it's both to varying degrees. There are indeed times when, in a fit of Borderline thinking, we will certainly lower ourselves to the childish tactic of "I hurt, so I'll make you hurt too," but there are also times when we are so terribly hurt by an experience that we cannot bear to face the person we blame for inflicting that pain upon us.

Why is my character flaw named Borderline Personality Disorder? I feel well over the border when it has become obvious to me that I've done something wrong or inappropriate.

I'd like to first clarify that this is not necessarily something I'd call a "character flaw." I'm not entirely sure why I'd like to reclassify that but "flaw" is such a negative term that I'm hesitant to use it, especially in this setting – where we're aiming for healthy, happy living.

I don't think there's any consensus in the mental health community about the origins of the term "borderline" but my personal thought on the subject is that since it is rare to find Borderline "standing alone", it's generally 'bordering' some accompanying disorder such as ADHD, PTSD, OCD or Bi-Polar, among the myriad of disorders out there. The traits from Borderline are so varied that they can easily mimic the symptoms from other disorders. They border many disorders so I'm guessing that might be where the term Borderline originated. But I could certainly be wrong!

Another take on the term could be that there is a lack of borders between the afflicted individual and those around them. We are generally incapable of separating our stuff from the stuff that rightly belongs to others, so the border lines are blurred or missing entirely.

I think it's when you've stepped over that line that's missing that you realize you've done something "wrong" and it's because the line – for you – is missing that brings about the phrase Borderline Personality Disorder.

Once you finally put aside the denial, and can see where the Borderline can set in (I mean to say that I don't think that my problems are constant, just stress related actually,) where do you start?

If this were a linear problem, something that could be accomplished by following a step-by-step set of instructions, I'd say "Start at the beginning." But since Borderline is similar to a swirling mass of emotions, feelings, thoughts and conflicting ideas and beliefs, it's virtually impossible to say, "Here, this is the starting point." Unfortunately, it's going to be one of those things where you'll end up dealing with multiple areas of your life and your disorder at the same time, feeling as though you're mastering none of the areas but slowly making progress in all of the areas.

If I were to make a suggestion, I'd say: pick the thing that stands out most in your mind right this moment.

No doubt I am wallowing in some self-pity. Yet my feelings are real to me, so real, I feel the way I do right now. My wife and son deeply resent me because they do not understand me.

I have no doubt whatsoever that your feelings are indeed very real to you - as they should be - however I'm challenging the basis of origination for those feelings. You say that your wife and son deeply resent you "because they do not understand" you and I challenge that. Is it possible that perhaps they deeply resent you for the actions you've taken in the past that have caused them pain, heartache, fear? Is it possible that perhaps they don't *deeply resent* you but that they are fearful and wary of your unpredictability? Is it possible that it's you who doesn't understand them and you're projecting your own deep-seated resentment of yourself onto them?

Sometimes it's more beneficial to look beyond the feelings and examine the root of them. When we sit there and wallow in self-pity because of this or that, yes the feelings are real but the reasons for them may not be. We may have twisted our thinking around which is resulting in these self-pitying feelings. What I'm asking in the questions of possibility above is that you examine the form and shape of the thinking that got you to this point of self-pity and then, ideally, work to untwist your thinking.

Believe me, I understand about feeling exhausted and frustrated about trying to make any real progress. When it feels like you're spinning your wheels, it probably means you don't have any traction. Time to get new wheels or put on chains or do something different from what you've been doing because continuing to do the same thing will always get you the same result. Don't try to overcome the *feelings* so much as try to overcome the *thinking* that gets you to those feelings!

In my recovery, I seem to make ground, feel like I am getting better then I fall back. Was this true of your recovery?

Most certainly, without a doubt and with no hesitation whatsoever! I constantly fought the feelings of "one step forward, seventeen steps backward." Each time I thought I had mastered some crucial aspect of healthy living, something else would come up and I'd be tossed about as if I were trying to ride a bull at a rodeo, indubitably ending up on my rump in a cloud of dust.

Part of the reason that putting this book together was so difficult for me was that there wasn't a simple set of instructions that I received that could be passed on in written format. My progress was never linear. I might get "better" at handling work stress but then a personal relationship would stumble and I would disintegrate completely. I would get extremely upset with myself for being such a ninny, for not being able to hold it together. After all, I had been able to put out sixteen fires in one day alone at the office and I felt comfortable and confident there but get me out of the office, and it was like I regressed to the whimpering child I always felt I was in my mother's presence.

As a wise young woman once told me, "It's not about how many times you fall off the horse, it's how many times you pick yourself up, dust yourself off and get back on that matter!"

Even though it may not seem as though you're making progress, especially during the beginning phases of recovery, there will come a point when you reflect back on the changes. What seems to be the most common is what I like to describe as the light-bulb effect when suddenly we realize, "Hey, six months ago, if she had said that to me, I would have flipped out completely. Now, I just chalked it up to her 'stuff' and moved on with my life. Way to go, Me!"

Because there are two hundred and fifty six types of Borderline, there cannot be a simple, linear set of recovery instructions that will be effective for all people attempting recovery. Rather, there are tools available to help you construct your own genuine self. By taking each tool out of its box, examining it carefully, practicing with it for a good long time and becoming comfortable using that tool, you then have the capability to handle any situation that arises. So what might feel like a backwards step or a failure to you at any given point is probably just the unfamiliarity of working with a new or different tool. Practice makes perfect and practice is what true recovery is all about!

I have stopped most of my acting out, but I still feel like I want to act out, I don't know what will replace the acting out if you see what I mean?

I generally recommend acting out in a constructive way:

- Join a martial arts class,
- Get a punching bag,
- Buy cheap pottery from a thrift store to smash and then make mosaic art, etc.

By doing something that's physically healthy, not destructive to the world around you (like destroying your antique china) and possibly even having something beautiful come out of your anger or frustration, you'll have more things to feel proud of down the road. Journal about how you felt during those times, what it felt like after the acting out, and how it feels to do something that's not destructive in a harmful way. Keep track of your progress.

Also, review the Five Steps. Re-work the homework exercises in that chapter. I think you'll find that as you become more comfortable in reviewing the options that are available to you at any given time, under any circumstance, you'll begin to find that "acting out" isn't the most desirable option. Over time, you'll find that "acting out" isn't even comfortable anymore.

I feel I should make my parents happy somehow. That's the way it's always been, from a very young age.

When you truly believe within your heart that YOU being genuinely happy is more important than making them – or anyone else – happy, you'll be free of Borderline. You should work on reprogramming those old tapes that have conditioned you to seek external validation and begin working on self-validating so that you become happy.

I guess one of the hardest things for me is wanting to feel close to people, but fearing the rejection, fearing the risk, and also that I am so bad that no one would genuinely like me.

Do YOU genuinely like you? Who IS the genuine you? Living in fear is one of those "comfortable knowns" that's like a giant tar pit. You know it's bad for you but you feel like it keeps you there because it's warm, it surrounds you, you haven't died yet...! Living in fear is not the way to live a healthy, happy life. What other fears have you overcome in your life? Fear of riding a bicycle for the first time? Fear of learning to swim? Fear of cooking for the first time? Focus on the positives that have resulted in your life as a result of overcoming your fears. Journal them, keep track, challenge yourself to overcome a different fear each month.

When you were working through your stuff and a lot of the past came up...

Actually, there wasn't a whole lot of the past that came up. It was more focused on the present because that was what my therapist believed in. The past cannot be changed; only the present and the future. It's like the Existential Paradox in The Angry Heart:

> *We are not responsible for how we came to be who we are as adults. But as adults we are responsible for whom we have become and for everything we do and say.*

Put another way, it doesn't make a whole lot of sense to sit down and try to figure out how you ended up lost in the woods without a map. The important thing is to get yourself out of the woods, alive and in one piece, so that you can get to a map and keep yourself from getting lost in there again.

Did you ever spiral into a self-destruction mode?

Many, many times. On a fairly regular basis. I broke up with Al every couple of weeks when we were first dating. The slightest little thing would send me into self-destruct mode.

Also, if so…how did you climb your way out?

For me, it was always cyclic in nature. That cycle went something like this:

He said something that enforced a boundary. I got in a tizzy because it triggered a slew of negative self-talk feelings I had all my life – generally from my childhood and basic fear of abandonment. I got into self-destruct mode because all I "knew" was that I didn't deserve anything good or worthwhile in my life so I may as well destroy it before it destroyed me. And then I'd sit there feeling sorry for myself, that life was so unfair, that I was all alone, that I was destined for misery and I'd realize that I'd pushed away someone who really cared about me. Oh, what I wouldn't give to make amends and get that happiness back, at whatever cost, for however long or short a period of time. And I'd come crawling back, begging for forgiveness, pleading for another chance.

My life was very much the "I hate you, don't leave me" refrain. It wasn't until I finally let it sink into my thick skull that I can't really control anyone else. If they want to leave me, they will – no matter what I say or do. I cannot control them; only myself.

I had to learn that it was okay to be angry or upset with someone else and just doing so wouldn't cause them to leave me. Sure, they might be angry in return but "all sickness ain't death."

You mentioned the past and basically I had to work really hard to erase the old tapes that used to play in my head that said I didn't deserve happiness. That said everyone would leave me. That said I was a loser and unlovable. I had to erase them because they were from the past. The words were spoken, but no one was saying them now. I had to stop living in the past and start shaping my present and aiming for the future I wanted.

I feel paralyzed to play this shit out...I am destroying my life here and my marriage.

Yeppers. When I was first dating my present husband, I was working at a job which was pretty stressful. I didn't have insurance yet, but I was very much in the throes of Borderline, though I didn't know it at the time. I was in mid-cycle and I was petrified. I wanted to talk to someone. I wanted to share what was going on in my head and heart. I was too scared to move. I was literally paralyzed with fear. I was scared to call him because I figured he'd think me a complete kook and decide I was too nutty to be with so I couldn't call him or else I'd wreck a potentially good relationship. I couldn't talk to my co-workers because I didn't want to be seen as they "psycho in payroll." I couldn't talk to my dad because he'd tell me it was a blood sugar issue. I had no one I could turn to and I was frozen with fear.

And there were plenty of times in therapy when your words came out of my mouth: "I can feel it's not right but I just can't stop myself." The truth of the matter was that I *could* stop myself, but at the time, I just didn't know HOW to stop myself. It wasn't until I really learned The Five Steps and put them into practice that I realized how much control over my life I really had.

It takes time, I won't lie. The path isn't linear, sometimes it's cyclic. The path isn't always smooth, sometimes it's back on the roller coaster. Sometimes it feels like you've climbed as far and as high as you possibly can and if you try to climb one more foot, your lungs will explode from the exertion. But you know what? It's okay to take a break once in a while, to catch your breath, to slide back down a few feet. If you learn from it or become stronger from it, you're ultimately helping yourself reach that pinnacle.

So... in a nutshell, I'd say it was The Five Steps that did it. Really and truly. But it was never a single light bulb moment, or one glorious morning where the world and I and myself finally made sense. It was a long, arduous process, fraught with the exact same doubts, fears and concerns you're expressing right now.

Do you want to lead a healthy, happy life? You have to truly commit to it. You have to be strong enough to admit when you screw up. You have to be tough enough to say to yourself, after you screw up, "Yeah, I screwed up, but I'm going to try again to get this right." You have to be willing to retrain your brain and erase the old tapes. You have to be willing to keep on fighting for the better life.

I have faith in you. The fact that you're reaching out, that you have awareness and (if I do say so myself) the fact that you sound just like I did... it shows me that you DO have what it takes to make it to healthy, happy living! Cut yourself some slack and & quit expecting yourself to suddenly be perfect overnight. It'll take time, patience and practice but it WILL happen – if you keep at it.

Once you finally put aside the denial, and can see where the Borderline can set in (I mean to say that I don't think that my problems are constant, just stress related actually) where do you start?

That's not a question that has only one right answer. Maybe my publisher would like it if I said the true first step to recovery is buying this book! But the honest answer is that the journey is different for every single person because we are all unique individuals with unique experiences, beliefs and goals. If I were to tell you to start at X because that's where I started, but maybe you would be better off starting at A, and someone else would be better off starting at L, then I would be hindering all of you rather than helping you.

A generic answer would be to read and learn all that you can about Borderline Personality Disorder. They say that knowledge is power and "they" are right! The more you know, the better informed your decision process will be, and the more likely you will be to make the "right" decisions for you and your situation and circumstances. I would also suggest that you keep your options and your mind open to all possibilities. Don't outright dismiss anything – medications, a specific type of therapy, a particular therapist, an online resource – because you don't know if it's for you unless you try it. And even when you try it or check into it and it doesn't feel perfectly right for you, you might be surprised later because if you stick it out, you might learn something about yourself that you hadn't expected.

I've said before that the journey to recovery isn't linear. There isn't a set of step-by-step instructions on how to overcome the Borderline stuff and begin leading a healthy, happy life. If there were, someone would have published that long before this book! I've tried to present the material in this book in as linear a fashion as was possible. It was no easy task because, by now, I'm sure you've noticed that virtually every topic is interrelated to at least one other topic in the book. If this book was too theoretical for you to pick out a specific starting point, then my advice is to pick any point and start there. Set an effective goal and do the work to achieve that goal. Draw on the knowledge you've gathered and give it a try.

I have BPD, and I was wondering if you could lead me in the right direction as far as therapy goes. My counselor doesn't help, and I have taken DBT classes which helped only a little. I am wondering if a residential type program is available that deals just with Borderlines, at a reasonable cost, and that is known to be beneficial when other things have failed.

Chapter Five discussed the three main types of therapeutic approaches: CBT, DBT and Psychoanalysis. If your counselor isn't helping you, stop going. Would you continue to run around the house as fast as possible if you knew it wasn't going to get your bed sheets changed? To me, that's just as absurd as continuing to see a therapist or counselor that isn't giving you what you need. You're wasting your time, the counselor's time and your money. I'm reminded of the joke where the guy goes to the doctor and says, "It hurts when I do this" and the doctor says, "Then stop doing that."

I encourage you to review Chapter Four – specifically the advice given about the role of the therapist. It's alright, as the buyer, to continue shopping until you find the right "product" for you.

As for the residential program, I would direct you to the Resources section at the back of this book and check through some of the listed areas of information. I have no personal familiarity with any residential programs and only peripheral knowledge of "The Angry Heart Clinic" run by Dr. Joseph Santoro in upstate New York, and I don't believe that would fall into the category of "reasonable cost" for most people's budgets.

I am wondering if I not only suffer from Bi-P, but from BPD as well. Is this common?

Yes, of course it's possible and it's very common. I don't have actual statistics to share with you – I can't say that x% of those diagnosed with Borderline will also be diagnosed with Bi-Polar – but I do know that it's fairly common based on my own experiences. I, myself, have a mild form of Bi-Polar and some of my friends have more pronounced forms of Bi-Polar along with their own Borderline stuff. BPD is common found co-morbid with other disorders and Bi-Polar is just one of many.

How do I present BPD to someone I care about as the basis of many of her problems so that she will at least consider it with an open mind when she now hates me and blames me for leaving her and everything else bad in her life?

Don't I have some obligation to at least pass this potential "key" along to someone who might be able to, metaphorically, slide it across the table to her at the right moment, should that moment ever arise?

If I understand the questions properly, you believe someone you know might have Borderline and you're wondering if you have some sort of obligation to share your belief with that person, or at the very least pass along your hypothesis to someone else who might share it with her at the right time.

Here's the thing: You can lead a horse to water and you can even build a jewel-encrusted trough and fill it with premium imported water but you still cannot force that horse to drink that water. Honestly, I would have been angry, very angry, if someone I knew – a layperson – tried to diagnose me with a personality disorder. The fact that I knew something was wrong with me, my life and my thought processes still doesn't mean I would have accepted a peer diagnosis with grace. I would have been angry that you thought you were better than me and felt superior to me. Even though you might have shared your thoughts and concerns with me out of love and compassion, all I would have heard from you is, "You're messed up and you need professional help."

Yes, I knew I needed professional help but by the same token, you're not a professional so you have no credentials or solid base of knowledge from which you could diagnose, let alone help, me. Furthermore, my own personal experience with professionals up to the point where I finally did get an accurate diagnosis was that the half-dozen professionals with whom I'd already consulted were obviously of marginal value to me because, years later, I was still not "fixed." And you have the audacity to claim that you know more than they do?

That said, I won't say that, unilaterally, no one should ever broach the subject of Borderline Personality Disorder with someone else. Under the right circumstances, I'm sure it's possible that it can be very beneficial and result in a life-changing course of events. I don't believe that there's ever an obligation for one person to share their opinion of BPD with another. One person's opinion is their stuff. Forcing that stuff onto another person is eerily similar to the melding of stuff as part of the inherent dynamic of Borderline.

Could you please inform me of resources discussing effects of BPD on the children in the household?

I would encourage you to review the areas of information listed in the Resources section at the back of this book for clinical and/or definitive studies on this topic.

Speaking as a layperson, I can honestly say that I think BPD begets BPD. That is, if a child is exposed to Borderline during their formative years and they have a genetic predisposition to a mood disorder or chemical imbalance, then I do believe it's highly likely that the child will have certain behavioral and psychological issues to overcome in later years that may otherwise not have been present. The reason I believe this is because children are sponges during their formative years. When they are taught – through example – that mind-reading is par for the course, that life is a seen in black-and-white terms, that life is lived on a roller coaster of ups and downs, that is what they will believe is "normal." They will grow up to emulate these things.

Do you think that parents who have BPD should not have children? Or that their children should be removed from their custody until they're better?

Not necessarily. I know quite a large number of parents who have Borderline. When their children were young – in the formative stages – the parents didn't know what Borderline was. So yes, there was a period of upheaval and uncertainty. When a parent with Borderline accepts their condition, moves out of denial and takes an active role in their own recovery, I think it's actually beneficial to the child to be around as the parent makes the strides toward a healthy, happy life. What better way for the child to learn the new and improved ways of life than from the same parent who taught them the chaotic, dramatic ways of Borderline?

My question is will and can she understand that I love her just for being herself, and is there any advice you can give me in terms of helping her get treatment?

I hate to be nit-picky about this but you cannot force someone else to get treatment. Well, I suppose under certain circumstances, it is possible to force someone into a facility designed to treat patients, but that is obviously no guarantee that the person will be receptive to the treatment being offered or that they will do the work that is required of them to make effective and lasting progress.

Yes, it is possible that the person you care about can and may some day understand that you do love her just as she is. For someone with Borderline, it's very hard for us to understand the distinction between "I love you" and "I don't like your behavior" because the second statement totally eradicates the first statement. My behavior is a reflection of who I am so if you don't like my behavior, it stands to reason that you don't like me. That must mean that you are a part-time liar so why should I believe anything you say?

I believe the key to salvaging interpersonal relationships is effective and consistent boundary enforcement. I often refer to this process as "giving a boundary sandwich." If you picture a rather plain sandwich consisting of a slice of bread, a slice of meat and another slice of bread, that's what I ask you to do when setting boundaries for the Borderline in your life.

> **Bread / Love:** I love you a great deal.
>
> **Meat / Boundary:** I won't put up with your temper tantrums. You need to leave until you can calm down.
>
> **Bread / Love:** You can come back when you're feeling better and we can talk. I love you.

The key to helping the Borderline in your life through this while maintaining your sanity and getting the relationship stable is going to be repeating boundaries. Pure and simple. Say it. Say it again. Say it again. Say it a few more times. Repeat yourself. Repeat yourself repeatedly. Repetitious repeating.

Consequences should be clear – or black-and-white – and they should be announced up-front. Don't try to surprise this person. If you're thinking that something could be a consequence, share that with the person. Allowing things to simmer under the surface while your blood begins to boil and then slapping them with an eruption and a rash consequence will simply add fuel to the Borderline fire. Instead, make your boundaries and consequences clear.

> **Boundary / Consequence:** If you raise your voice to me or throw a single thing in a fit of anger, you will be asked to leave. You'll be able to come back when you can conduct yourself in a rational, adult manner. The choice of how you act is completely up to you. If you'd like to discuss X topic with me, you will do so without screaming or throwing things. If you can't do that, you'll need to leave. Do you understand?

Lather, rinse, repeat. You will need to make these consequences to actions perfectly clear. By expressing them in a format that is easily understood to a Borderline mind – in black-and-white – the person you care about will, over time, begin to see the steady pattern they've never before encountered in their life. Things are suddenly predictable to them. The chaos has been transformed to understandable, logical, black-and-white consequences to actions.

But you've said that black-and-white thinking was wrong so why should I try to reinforce that thought process to the Borderline in my life?

Actually, I spent a good portion of Chapter Fifteen discussing how the black-and-white thinking could be turned into an advantage and a tool for recovery from BPD. The ultimate goal of recovery work is to see the world in shades of grey – and all other colors, of course. But in order to be able to do that, the chaos inside the Borderline mind must first be ordered into logical, rational, understandable groupings of black-and-white consequences to actions and boundaries. When that work has been done, and while it's in process, there will be some areas which overlap or are in direct opposition to other aspects. This is usually one of the more difficult things for a recovering Borderline to reconcile: duality.

If the answer to one question is black and the answer to a similar question is white, which one is right?

The answer is: both are right. The answer to both is grey. The moment you (as the one with Borderline) can see and understand that enigma, the rest will fall into place naturally. You'll suddenly have this tremendous frame of reference for understanding grey. This moment will be your own light bulb.

I'm ending the relationship. Can I have any peace of mind that my no longer enabling her bad behavior will be more loving to her than if I had stayed for more abuse?

This is a tough one. It seems the question is asking for absolution for action. I cannot provide that to you. As with any situation, there are a great number of possible outcomes. It seems that your desired outcome is that, by removing your presence, and subsequent enabling, this woman will be seen as the more loving gesture than if you had stayed by her side.

I would hope that more people would chose to stay in a relationship they believed in and support the person they loved in a healthy and effective manner. If you feel you are unable to provide that healthy and effective support, then yes, I would say it's probably for the best that you disengage from the relationship.

It takes two to tango.

While Borderline Personality Disorder is something that emanates from within the afflicted individual, if that person is presented with the "relationship rules" which would prohibit their acting out, the other person, in essence, changes the tune to which the pair had previously been dancing. The person with Borderline then has to decide if they wish to dance to the new tune, say a fox trot or a jitterbug. If they opt out of the relationship because they do not want to dance to that new tune, then I would say you would have peace of mind insofar as you had done the most loving thing possible: you had offered her an opportunity to learn a new dance. That is to say, you'd offered the healthy and effective boundaries and consequences to having a healthy, adult relationship.

By simply walking away, what have you taught? That if the tune is undesirable, just walk away. This is already the trend of the Borderline way of coping.

If you are unable to commit to learning new ways of setting boundaries and limits and are unable to impose and follow-through on effective consequences to actions, then, for both of your sakes, it probably is best that you end the relationship because neither of you is positioned to learning healthier ways of conducting your individual selves, let alone working together to create a healthy, adult relationship. Two wrongs don't make it right. If one of you is on the right path and offer to help guide the other, then I would predict the possibility of a successful outcome. If both of you are unable to see the healthy alternatives, then you're both simply perpetuating the "wrongs" of the relationship and, in that case, yes, I think it would be best to call it quits.

Could you suggest any clinical trials or research going on regarding new BPD diagnoses?

Because I'm not a clinician, I have studiously avoided aligning myself with anything of a clinical nature. There are some areas that might be of interest to you in the Resources section of this book. I believe one site in particular has a vast collection of resources on this very topic.

Appendix A – Contracts

Since Borderline includes a lot of black-and-white thinking, it stands to reason that entering into a contract would work quite well. For some people, contracts are a saving grace. We offer a few of them herein and also on the accompanying CD for ease of customization and reuse.

A Contract With and For Myself

I, _____, am making the following contract with myself to control self-destructive and disruptive behavior in the future.

This contract will provide clear guidelines for my behavior, especially for when I am angry, upset, or depressed.

The purpose of this contract is to help me allow others to help me and to help me help myself. I have the right to be safe from myself. If I know that I am not safe, I will go to an appropriate inpatient psychiatric facility where I can be safe, and I will stay there until I am ready to leave and be safe outside the facility. I will remember that_____ is an outpatient facility and has limited services. I will go there only for the following reasons:

- Appointment with counselor

- Appointment with psychiatrist

- Change of appointment/make new appointment with secretary

My counselor has other clients and a life outside his/her work. I will contact my counselor outside appointments only concerning appointment times [note: this can be defined with the signer and the counselor to reflect a more personal schedule which may include going for emergencies (with the emergency counselor on call and only for 15 minutes and only for an assessment for safety) and/or sending one letter or email per week]. If I have thoughts or ideas between appointments that I wish to share with my counselor, I will write them down or type them and bring them to my next appointment.

Safety

If I am safe but unable to function as expected of me as a student or professional, I will go home for an appropriate length of time. The purpose of this trip will not be to escape my problems but to have time away from stress and to regroup. In other words, I will enjoy myself and be good company to those around me, but I will also think about returning and functioning and using the resources available to me. I will be honest (with (those around me who, that care about me, who are part of my support system) about how I am feeling when I am at home and let them help me if I need help.

Medications

- I will take any medication prescribed to me (unless I know that I am allergic or will have a bad reaction), and I will take it as prescribed.

- I will cooperate with my psychiatrist and inform him/her how I feel about my medication and/or treatment plan.

- I will ask him/her any questions that I may have until I feel satisfied with the answers.

- I will contact my counselor and/or parents/friends/support system and/or home doctor if I am at all uncomfortable with anything related to my medication but am unable to resolve the issue with my psychiatrist.

- I will inform an appropriate person if I feel I am having a reaction to my medication.

Contractual Behaviors/Actions

I will avoid certain actions in order to help myself:

- I will not bang my head.

- I will not hit the wall or other hard surface with any other part of my body.

- I will not throw hard or heavy objects.

- I will not intentionally break objects.

Appendix A

- I will not intentionally cut myself or prick myself with any object.
- I will not purposely deprive myself of food or sleep.
- I will not consume my bodily fluids.
- I will not remain alone for longer than 15 minutes when I am thinking about hurting myself (being on the phone or online with somebody counts as not being alone).
- I will not spend more than 30 minutes at a time alone in the bathroom (or any other place where my mind or body is not occupied) at a time.
- I will not spend more than an hour and a half in that situation per day.
- I will not contact anyone who does not wish to be contacted by me or attempt to find out information about a person to use in an inappropriate way.
- I will not contact a person when I know it is not appropriate or think it may not be appropriate.
- I will not try to frighten anyone or try to take away a person's sense of security by any means.
- I will not stalk anybody.
- I will not make direct or implied threats or take actions upon myself to try to force a person to "rescue me" or make some certain action.
- I will be honest and cooperative with people who are trying to help me.
- If I realize that I am not honest or cooperative or am "playing games", I will inform the person I am involved with and stop immediately.
- I will take time alone if I need it in order to stop.
- If I act better or worse than I feel or less capable than I am in order to get attention or a certain response from a person or group of people, that is considered "playing games".
- If somebody deems to be a possible threat to myself or others, he/she must take certain action regardless of whether I claim to have been dishonest, uncooperative, or playing games.
- I will allow my counselor to be in contact with my parents/significant other when necessary, and I will trust the counselor on when it is necessary.
- I will keep my parents/significant other updated on my overall mood and general progress in counseling and what is happening with my medication. I need not tell them specifics about my mood or counseling, but I will be clear about what is going on with my medication.

Other/Additional:

I am responsible for my actions. If I decide not to take responsibility for my actions, then I will lose my right to make certain decisions.

If I break this contract in any way, it does not give me the right to continue breaking it.

I will not become discouraged or lose hope. Rather, I will become more determined to keep this contract.

I will inform my counselor if I break any part of the contract (and I will not break any part of the contract just to be able to tell my counselor about it), but I know that it is not the counselor's or anybody else's responsibility to make sure that I keep it. It is mine and mine only.

This contract will be in effect for _____ days, until _____ (date).

_____   _____
Signed by: Date

_____   _____
Witnessed by: Date

A Contract With and For Myself
An Addendum

I will follow the guidelines in My Contract With and For Myself for my behavior, and I understand that I am still responsible for the consequences of not following that contract.

I will focus on achieving the following _____ (number) goals between now and _____ (date):

Use appropriate coping techniques whenever I find myself obsessing about suicide, hurting myself, or doing any other behaviors that violate My Contract With and For Myself, and whenever I find myself doing or wanting to do behaviors that are on the list of unhealthy coping mechanisms.

Cope with (and lessen, if possible) the anxiety that I am and will be feeling about:

_____ using healthy coping methods.

_____.

_____.

_____.

_____.

I will not commit suicide before _____ (date).

I will try my best not to consider suicide as an option. Rather, I will focus on making progress in becoming a healthy adult.

This addendum contract will be in effect for _____ days, until _____ (date).

_____ _____
Signed by: Date

_____ _____
Witnessed by: Date

Family Contract

NAMES OF THOSE ENTERING INTO THE CONTRACT:

_____ _____ _____

_____ _____ _____

Basic Agreement

We understand that this contract will remain in effect for a minimum of _____ days after which time it may be re-negotiated at the request of one or more of the above. Following the re-negotiation, the contract should stay in effect for a minimum of _____ days.

This contract is being entered into in a spirit of cooperation and understanding in the belief that it will benefit all parties.

This contract is divided into three parts:

- Responsibilities
- Consequences
- Privileges

RESPONSIBILITIES:

What is expected of the adolescent and family members.

CONSEQUENCES:

What will occur if the responsibilities are not maintained.

PRIVILEGES:

The "rewards" earned by the adolescent when responsibilities are maintained to the extent that they satisfy the intentions of the contract.

Responsibilities

Communication

Adolescent agrees to relate to parent(s)/guardian(s) in a civil, considerate and respectful manner. _____ Agree _____ Disagree

ALL PARTIES AGREE THAT THERE WILL BE NO NAME CALLING, NO PHYSICAL THREATS OR USE OF PHYSICAL VIOLENCE, NO SARCASM AND NO USE OF DISRESPECT. ALL PARTIES ARE TO TREAT EACH OTHER THE SAME WAY THAT THEY WOULD WANT TO BE TREATED.

This does not mean that all parties will agree on every issue every time. *Disagreement does not mean disrespect.* The manner in which discussion is held is of importance.

School

Adolescent agrees to attend school and not skip classes. ____ Yes ____ No

Adolescent agrees to complete class work and homework assignments. ____ Yes ____ No

Adolescent agrees to study during the following time periods:

   From _____ to _____

   And from _____ to _____

   On the following days: _____

Adolescent agrees to maintain good behavior in school.
_____ Agree _____ Disagree

Adolescent agrees to maintain passing grades.
_____ Agree _____ Disagree

Curfew

Adolescent agrees to the following curfews:

SCHOOL YEAR:

   Weekdays: (Sunday – Thursday)

   Curfew is: _____

   Weekends: (Friday & Saturday)

   Curfew is: _____

SUMMER:

   Weekdays: (Sunday – Thursday)

   Curfew is: _____

   Weekends: (Friday & Saturday)

   Curfew is: _____

Curfew for special events will be discussed with parents/guardians IN ADVANCE of even and curfew decided upon.

Phone Use:

Adolescent agrees to the following conditions pertaining to use of the family phone:

Adolescent may use the phone for (specified amount of time):
_____

Between the hours of _____ and _____ on weeknights

Between the hours of _____ and _____ on weekends.

Adolescent agrees to disengage from phone conversations when other family members receive or need to place a call in a timely and courteous manner.

The adolescent will not run up long distance bills and will not make long distance calls without first asking permission.
_____ Agree _____ Disagree

Other family rules regarding use of phone:

_____
_____
_____
_____

Driving:

The adolescent realizes that driving is a PRIVILEGE AND NOT A RIGHT. Until the age of 17, the parent/guardian essentially OWNS the adolescent's drivers license. Appropriate use of vehicles and traffic laws will be followed whether the vehicle belongs to adolescent or parent/guardian (or someone else.)

The following rules apply to driving:

_____
_____
_____
_____

Appendix A 205

Privacy:

MOST IMPORTANTLY, ALWAYS TO BE REMEMBERED, PRIVACY IS CONDITIONAL!

As long as the adolescent is not suspected of endangering self or others – i.e. drug/alcohol use, promiscuous sex, suicidal thoughts/behaviors, aggressive behaviors, then parents/guardians will respect the adolescent's right to privacy – i.e. no listening on telephone conversations, reading letters/notes, rummaging through adolescent's belongings.

IF, HOWEVER, the adolescent exhibits any of the above behaviors, then the parent/guardian is acting in the best interest of the adolescent by attempting to discover the truth about the adolescent's activities.

Friends and Dating:

Adolescent agrees to avoid alcohol/drug using friends as much as possible: or friends otherwise engaged in illegal activities. These people include specifically:

_____

_____

_____

Adolescent agrees to bring friends to meet parent/guardian. Parent/guardian agrees to meet friends. Adolescent agrees to obtain permission for friends to visit and agrees to keep bedroom door open when friends visit the house unless given special permission. _____ Yes _____ No

Adolescent agrees to provide parents with phone numbers of friends (or location where he/she can be reached) and directions to the homes of friends. _____ Agree _____ Disagree

Adolescent agrees that when plans are made to go out that he/she will stick to those plans and IF plans are changed (location, activity, etc.) then adolescent will phone parent/guardian to notify and ask permission for change BEFORE MAKING ANY CHANGE IN PLANS.
_____ Agree _____ Disagree

Adolescent agrees that abstinence is the only "safe" sex. (This means NOT engaging in sexual activity.) _____ Agree _____ Disagree

Adolescent agrees to try to make the best choice for him/herself regarding sexual activity WITH HEALTH AND SAFETY THE PRIORITY! IF the adolescent chooses to engage in sexual relationships anyway, he/she agrees to accept responsibility for these actions by using appropriate protection in the form of condoms and birth control. _____ Agree _____ Disagree

Work (job outside the home):

Adolescent may seek, obtain and maintain full/part-time employment during the specified times and dates:

_____

_____

_____

Special conditions regarding use of adolescent's paycheck:

If adolescent has vandalized property or through misbehavior cost the parents/guardians money, then the adolescent agrees to pay for the damages in the amount of $_____ to be paid in installments of $_____ every _____week(s.)

If the adolescent has special expenses (example: car insurance) list these expenses:

_____

_____

_____

Music:

Adolescent agrees to keep the volume of music at a level acceptable to parent(s)/guardian(s) and agrees to abide by the following time limitations:

    Weekdays (Sunday – Thursday): _____

    Weekends (Friday & Saturday): _____

Smoking:

Adolescent is is NOT permitted to smoke.

If the adolescent is permitted to smoke, the following restrictions and limitations will be maintained:

_____

_____

_____

Illegal Activity:

The adolescent understands that the parent(s)/guardian(s) AGREE TO CHARGE AND AID IN THE PROSECUTION OF ANY AND ALL ILLEGAL ACTS.

Sobriety:

Adolescent agrees to abstain from the use of alcohol and other drugs.
_____ Agree   _____ Disagree

Adolescent agrees to inform parent(s)/guardian(s) if use does occur.

Adolescent agrees to NEVER RIDE IN OR DRIVE a vehicle with anyone under the influence or while under the influence of alcohol or any other drugs.

Adolescent agrees to call parent(s)/guardian(s) for a ride if ever in such a situation.

Parent(s)/guardian(s) agree to pick the adolescent up and discuss the situation calmly.

IF the adolescent is under the influence of drugs/alcohol, then parent(s)/guardian(s) will wait until adolescent is sober to discuss situation.

IF adolescent continually has to call for a ride, then parent(s)/guardian(s) will have to evaluate the situation of use and/or friends.
_____ Agree   _____ Disagree

Adolescent agrees to random testing to alcohol and drugs if this has been or becomes and issue in adolescent's life.   _____ Agree   _____ Disagree

Chores:

Adolescent agrees to maintain at least those "common" areas of the house in a neat and orderly manner, according to the standards of the home.

Adolescent agrees to clean up own messes and so forth. (It is recommended that adolescent be allowed to keep bedroom as wished short of health or safety hazards.)

Additionally, adolescent agrees to do certain designated chores as listed below:

_____

_____

_____

_____ Agree   _____ Disagree

Other Responsibilities and/or Agreements:

We, the adolescent and parent(s)/guardian(s) agree to consistently maintain the following:

AfterCare: ☐

Family Therapy: ☐

Medications: ☐

AA/NA: ☐

_____

_____

_____

_____

_____

CONSEQUENCES

Communications:

**If disrespect enters into any discussion or interaction, conversation will immediately come to an end.

If the disrespect is on the part of the adolescent, any request of favor will be automatically dismissed.

If the disrespect is on the part of the parent(s)/ guardian(s), they agree to stop talking for a period of five (5) minutes and to listen attentively to the adolescent's presentation.

The above condition will be maintained in any interaction between persons in the home.

This is not to be interpreted as a "gag" device. Expressions of anger are not, in and of themselves, expressions of disrespect and should not be so interpreted. SARCASM, VIOLENCE – IMPLIED OR REAL, NAME CALLING, EXTREME RAISING OF THE VOICE (LOUD, PROLONGED SHOUTING) ARE DISRESPECTFUL.

Appendix A 209

School:

If school is skipped or classes are cut, the following consequences will go into effect:

_____

_____

_____

Homework and class work are to be completed per the agreement. Failure to do so will result in loss of privileges and/or the following consequences:

_____

_____

_____

Curfew:

If a curfew violation occurs, consequences will be imposed during a similar time period as the occurrence.

Example: If the violation occurs on a weeknight, the penalty will be imposed on the next weeknight.

Example: If the violation occurs on a weekend night, the penalty will be imposed on the next weekend night.

The penalty is established on a ratio of two-to-one (2:1).

Example: If the adolescent is late 5 – 30 minutes, then the penalty shall be a sixty (60) minute earlier curfew for the next night.

Example: If the adolescent is 31 – 60 minutes late, then the penalty shall be two (2) hours earlier the next night.

Anything over one hour shall result in the loss of going-out privileges for the next two (2) nights.

Curfew will not conflict with those established by Probation or other law enforcement agencies.

Staying out overnight will only occur after parental permission has been established, preferably IN ADVANCE OF GOING OUT.

Additionally:

_____

_____

_____

Phone:

Misuse or violation of phone privileges will result in the loss of phone use for a period of _____ days.

Continued violation of phone use will result in the following restrictions:

_____

_____

_____

Driving:

If the adolescent breaks a traffic law, the adolescent shall, at the very best pay the fine for said violation.

Further, depending on the seriousness of the violation, the adolescent may lose driving privileges at parent(s)/guardian(s) discretion.

DRIVING WHILE UNDER THE INFLUENCE OF DRUGS OR ALCOHOL, WHETHER OR NOT THE ADOLESCENT RECEIVES A LEGAL CONSEQUENCE, SHALL RESULT IN THE LOSS OF DRIVING PRIVILEGES FOR _____ (specify time period) EVEN IF ADOLESCENT OWNS HIS/HER OWN VEHICLE!

Failure to operate family vehicle in a manner that maintains safety and convenience of other family members (i.e. bringing car home "on empty" (no gas), trash filled, etc.) will result in the loss of use of family vehicle for _____ (specify time period.)

Privacy:

If adolescent is exhibiting dangerous behavior of any type, parent(s)/guardian(s) may do whatever is necessary to discover the true nature of adolescent activities.

Friends:

If any of the agreements are not followed, parent(s)/guardian(s) will restrict association with friends in question.

And/or the following restrictions will apply:

_____

_____

_____

Appendix A 211

Work (job outside the home):

The adolescent will live up to specifications of contract or lose the privilege of holding a job.

School attendance and passing grades must be maintained in order to continue working, especially during the school year.

Music:

Playing of music in a manner that disturbs other family members or violates contract will result in loss of use of music equipment for a period of _____ days.

Continued violation will result in the loss of the following privileges:

_____

_____

_____

Smoking:

If adolescent is allowed smoking privileges and violates the restrictions, the adolescent will lose smoking privileges for one week for the first violation.

If adolescent continues to violate smoking restrictions, permanent loss of privileges will occur.

If adolescent is NOT allowed to smoke and violates this agreement, loss of other privileges as follows will occur:

_____

_____

_____

Illegal Activity:

PARENT(S)/GUARDIAN(S) WILL AID IN THE PROSECUTION OF ANY ILLEGAL ACTIVITY.

212 Putting The Pieces Together

Sobriety:

If alcohol or other drug use occurs, the adolescent will:

_____
_____
_____
_____

The parent(s)/guardian(s) will:

_____
_____
_____
_____

Should the adolescent continue to use, the adolescent will:

_____
_____
_____
_____

Actions taken by the parent(s)/guardian(s) will:

_____
_____
_____
_____

And/or the following restrictions will apply:

_____
_____
_____

Privileges

- ☐ Special Lessons
- ☐ Auto/Driving
- ☐ Overnights
- ☐ Special Meals
- ☐ Allowance
- ☐ Concerts
- ☐ Peers/Friends
- ☐ Redo Room
- ☐ Dating
- ☐ Gifts
- ☐ Trips
- ☐ Other

Please explain items checked above: (include information about when, where and with whom)

_____
_____
_____
_____
_____
_____
_____
_____
_____
_____
_____
_____
_____
_____
_____
_____
_____

Putting The Pieces Together

Appendix B – Support Networks & Resources

It must be understood that no promises nor guarantees can be made with respect to the information or support provided at the sources of support listed in this chapter. This is primarily a collection of information which may, or may not, be helpful to you during your journey of recovery.

Resources

Helen's World of BPD Resources – http://www.bpdresources.com/ – A full website designed to be a store information relating to mental health, specifically BPD, and covers virtually every source on the internet. It's a very comprehensive and thorough site, maintained regularly.

Support Networks

Unfortunately, there isn't much in the way of national or worldwide in-person support networking, like one might find for Alcoholics Anonymous. The list below offers a wide selection of online support networking.

- BPDRecovery.com – http://www.bpdrecovery.com – A full website created by the author of this book, dedicated to offering assistance to those interested in recovering from BPD. There is a very active discussion board for all people who are interested in healthier, happier living – regardless of diagnosis. It is an open community and you needn't be a registered member to participate.

- Without Borders – http://p207.ezboard.com/bwithoutborders5000 – An active discussion board for anyone with Borderline Personality Disorder. The community was originally founded by a woman from Canada. While she still participates from time to time, she has passed along the torch to some of the other community members.

- BPDCentral.com – http://www.bpdcentral.com – A full website created by the author of "Stop Walking On Eggshells." **WARNING** This site is designed for the support of those in relationships with someone who has BPD. Many with Borderline find the information and discussion board to be too much to take early on in the process. Use extreme caution before proceeding to this site!

- The Shack – http://www.mjtacc.com/ – A full website hosted and designed for Australians. The site is segmented into two areas: those who do and those who do not have BPD. The community is moderately active.

- BPD from the Inside Out – http://www.borderlinepersonality.org/ – A full website hosted by A.J. Mahari, a prolific columnist about the subject of BPD, also recovered and Canadian. The community is moderately active but may occasionally lack focus as the community doesn't really have leadership.

- Mental Earth – http://www.mentalearth.com/ – A discussion forum that is very active and covers a broad spectrum of mental health issues.

Appendix C – Acronyms & Definitions

APD – Avoidant Personality Disorder

BiPD – Bi-Polar Disorder, formerly known as Manic Depression

BiP – someone who suffers Bi-Polar Disorder

BPD – Borderline Personality Disorder

BP – someone who suffers Borderline Personality Disorder

CBT – Cognitive Behavior Therapy

DBT – Dialectical Behavior Therapy

DID – Dissociative Identity Disorder, formerly known as Multiple Personality Disorder (MPD)

Dx – Diagnosis

Meds – Medications – generally those medications prescribed for mental health conditions.

MI – Mental Illness

NPD – Narcissistic Personality Disorder

OCD – Obsessive Compulsive Disorder

P-Doc – Psychiatrist – a doctor who has passed the med

PD – Personality Disorder

218 Putting The Pieces Together

Pdoc – psychiatrist, capable of prescribing meds

PTSD – Post-Traumatic Stress Disorder

PMDD – PreMenstrual Dysphoric Disorder

SI – Self-Injury

T – Therapist – a psychologist, licensed clinical social worker or licensed counselor whose primary role is to talk about issues with the patient,

220 Putting The Pieces Together

Sources

"The Four Agreements: A Practical Guide to Personal Freedom" by Miguel Ruiz, published by Amber-Allen Publishing, November 1997, ISBN 1878424319

"I Hate You, Don't Leave Me: Understanding Borderline Personality Disorder" by Jerold J. Kreisman and Hal Straus, published by Avon, February 1991, ISBN 0380713055

"The Feeling Good Handbook" by David D. Burns, published by Plume, December 1999, ISBN 0452281326

"Dark Moon Mysteries: Wisdom, Power, and Magic of the Shadow World" by Timothy Roderick (author) and Anthony Meadows (illustrator), published by Llewellyn Publications, June 1996, ISBN 156718345X

222 Putting The Pieces Together

Verona Publishing, Inc.
P.O. Box 24071
Edina, Minnesota 55424

www.veronapublishing.com

224 Putting The Pieces Together